the wagamama cookbook

Hugo Arnold

the
wagamama
cookbook

100 japanese recipes with noodles and much more

Hugo Arnold

METRO BOOKS
NEW YORK

This 2010 edition published by Metro Books, by arrangement with Kyle Cathie Ltd.

Author Hugo Arnold   **Project editor** Sarah Epton   **Photographer** Deirdre Rooney   **Art direction and design** Vanessa Courtier   **Food stylist** Joss Herd   **Props stylist** Wei Tang   **Copy editor** Stephanie Horner   **Editorial assistant** Vicki Murrell   **Production** Sha Huxtable and Alice Holloway

Front cover photograph © Judah Passow
Photography © 2004 wagamama limited
Hugo Arnold is hereby identified as the author of this work in accordance with Section 77 of the Copyright, Designs and Patents Act 1988

Metro Books
122 Fifth Avenue
New York, NY 10011

ISBN: 978-1-4351-2943-6

A Catalog In Publication record for this title is available from the Library of Congress.

Printed and bound in Singapore by Tien Wah Press

10 9 8 7 6 5 4 3 2 1

All recipes serve 2 people unless otherwise stated

contents

introduction

It is 2:30 on a sunny May afternoon and the original wagamama in Streatham Street in London is full. People are still arriving for late lunches, although the line is not nearly as long as it was an hour ago. On the table next to me are two lovers on their first date. Opposite, a group of eight students sit in animated conversation while up from them an elderly couple hold hands while they drink glasses of raw juice.

My order arrives: *yaki soba* noodles along with a side order of duck *gyoza*, dumplings filled with succulent meat and leeks served with a sweet hoisin dipping sauce. I hear the students all order by number; five of them go for 77, the others select a 71, a 103, and a 76. These are among the most popular dishes. When the second London wagamama opened in Lexington Street in Soho in 1996, somebody made the mistake of altering a few of the numbers. It caused *great* confusion.

Wagamama first opened its doors to the public in 1992. Since then it has spawned numerous outlets in countries as far apart as Ireland, Holland and Australia and for many—including me—it has redefined the idea of casual eating. The dishes are designed for one-stop eating. I order "sides" because I'm hungry. Many don't bother and the bill consequently remains remarkably low and very controllable. At wagamama, what you order is very plainly what you pay for. There are no hidden extras.

I pick up my chopsticks and start to eat my teppan-fried *yaki soba* noodles. The dish is a treasure trove of ingredients: egg, chicken, shrimp, onions, peppers, and bean sprouts topped with sesame seeds, dried shallots, and pickled ginger. The ice-cold Asahi beer hits the back of my throat and I'm feeling very content.

Cooking noodles is easy; this is what lies behind the success of wagamama. A combination of fresh and staple ingredients, delivered swiftly in a range of delicious ways, and presented stylishly. Perfect for the home cook, too, in our time-starved age, which is the reason for this book. Preparation time required for most of the dishes is well within 15 minutes and most are cooked in under ten, many in less than five. Considering that the bulk of the ingredients could be sitting in your cupboard at home gives you the added attraction of convenience.

I finish my *yaki soba* and ask for the bill. My waitress, a young student it turns out, in her final year at college and studying physics, chats away as she keys my request into her hand-held computer. As we talk, two more students arrive to join the eight who have already ordered. In less than 30 seconds their order—given by number, of course—is keyed in and soon they are catching up with their friends over bowls of steaming *ramen* noodles. My bill arrives and in moments I am up on the street again in brilliant sunshine, feeling well fed and refreshed for a very reasonable amount of money.

When wagamama started, nothing like it existed. Founder Alan Yau had considerable difficulty persuading anyone that a large basement site behind the British Museum had a chance of surviving, let alone succeeding. Yet he had a vision and determination not only to serve fast, nutritious, Asian-inspired cuisine, but to do so in a stark, restrained, and ultramodern environment. Some of the wagamama restaurants undoubtedly are "softer" than others—there is more use of wood in some of the more recent ones, for example—but they all retain a definite clean, pared-back look that allows customers and staff alike to provide the action and warmth.

Back in my flat the following day I am testing the *cha han*—one of the most popular dishes—for a group of friends. I have been asked by wagamama to write a cookbook explaining the company's approach to cooking noodles and Asian food and how easy this is to achieve at home. For a year I have been immersed in noodle dishes, the workings of a dynamic and growing company, and a group of highly motivated, hard-working people. I am experiencing the way of the noodle.

The recipes in the book are specified for two people on the basis that you can easily scale up if necessary; I am cooking for six. My friends have all offered to bring beer, so my shopping trip was limited to buying chicken and mushrooms. Soon I am chopping and putting ingredients into bowls. By the time I have cooked the rice, everything is cleared up and people arrive. We sit drinking cold beers and chatting. I have to use two frying pans—to see if the recipe will work without a wok—yet I am in the kitchen for less than 10 minutes (the recipe does work).

All the dishes at wagamama are designed to use a set number of ingredients. That is part of the reason why the service is so fast. Wagamama has redefined the expression "fast food"; taking fresh, nutritious ingredients, cooking them well, and delivering them efficiently. For the home cook this means you don't need to keep a lot in stock, and shopping is very easy. The whole style of cooking concentrates on intense heat, applied for a short period, letting the ingredients shine through and ensuring the cook doesn't spend forever in the kitchen. With these recipes, a sharp knife, a cutting board, and a wok, you, too, can cook the wagamama way.

1
the wagamama kitchen

The wagamama restaurant kitchens are organized so that any item on an order goes to one station where it is prepared. The dish is then put up on the "pass" where it is collected and brought to your table. When you are cooking at home, you are more likely to be preparing a number of dishes together. The key thing to bear in mind is that not much cooking takes place until the last moment. It can seem as if you are chopping and sorting for ages with little to show for your efforts. While this may at first be frustrating, in the end it is part of what makes this cooking so easy.

In the early days of wagamama, much was made of the Japanese management system of *kaizen*, which means continuous improvement or, as chief executive Ian Neill would say, you do something, learn something, do some more things. As with *kaizen* culture, you are using little stages to build the final assembly. Whichever way you choose to explain it, the idea is to chip away and move forward—that way you learn.

Many of the recipes in this book have appeared on the wagamama menu at some time or other. There is nothing complicated or difficult about cooking any of them. We excluded a few of the deep-fried dishes on the grounds that most people don't want to do too much deep frying in their own kitchen and some recipes have been altered slightly to cater for a domestic environment, but in essence they retain the same characteristics as the day they made it through a tasting and onto the wagamama menu.

the equipment

There is no need to go out and buy any special equipment. A wok will make things easier—they are not expensive (best bought from Asian stores)—but a large, nonstick frying pan will suffice. Chopsticks will enhance the eating experience, but a fork is fine. *Ramen* bowls are useful if you are going to cook this kind of food frequently. They are quite large, to accommodate the broth, and tend to be made from a material that insulates the heat so you can pick them up. They are, however, quite expensive. It's best to experiment with the things you already have, initially, and indulge on more expensive equipment later; that way you'll know exactly what you want and why. The one piece of kitchen equipment we did worry about was the teppan, a large flat plate on which the Japanese fry noodles mixed with other ingredients. Yet a heavy nonstick frying pan is a perfectly good substitute at home.

Wagamama sells a limited number of items which may be useful for cooking and presenting some of the dishes in this book. These include: *ramen* bowls, *cha han* bowls, wooden *ramen* ladles, sake jugs and cups, *gyoza* trays, and *miso* cups and lids. Woks, knives, bowls, and chopsticks are all readily found in Asian food stores.

stir-frying—an art or a secret?

While a frying pan can be used instead of a wok, you'll quite quickly discover that the shape and heat dispersal of a wok are unique. And that there is a world of difference between frying and stir-frying, which lies in the speed and temperature at which you cook. Tossing food around in a wok may seem a daunting and challenging way of cooking. A degree of technique and skill must be learned and applied, but it is not as difficult as you may think. Once mastered, it's a dazzling way of impressing your dinner guests and creating some really tasty food to eat.

Wok cooking is about speed. You want to cook the ingredients quickly and preserve as much nutritional value as possible. To do this, you must have heat—and lots of it.

In the wagamama kitchens we have the luxury of custom-made wok ranges which burn gas in a swirling motion, encouraging the flames to cover the whole bottom of the wok and not simply fire into one concentrated area. This helps to ensure an even heat distribution over the wok and eliminates any "cold spots." The average household does not possess such equipment, although there are now gas stovetops which incorporate a central "wok burner." Electric, halogen, and ceramic stovetops are less suited to using a wok than gas stoves, owing to the large amount of movement required during stir-frying, which reduces the contact with the heat source. This is where the large nonstick frying pan comes into its own. The larger the better, because the greater the surface area, the larger the area in contact with the gas flames so, the better the result.

Before stir-frying, be sure you have everything you need at hand: all the prepared ingredients, including seasonings, and warmed serving bowls or plates. It is essential to heat the wok thoroughly for 1–2 minutes before adding any oil, otherwise the wok will never get hot enough.

The process of stir-frying basically relies on movement. Movement is achieved using either a wok scoop, wooden spoon or spatula, or even chopsticks. You also need to move the wok itself to ensure even heat distribution. The wok can be "flicked" to move the ingredients around. This is best practiced in a cold wok with some raw rice. Tilt the wok lightly away from yourself, gently push forward, and then flick your wrist back. This movement causes the ingredients to move to the far edge of the wok and then be "flicked" back towards you. It is about action, not muscle, and with patience and practice, a basic level of skill can be mastered. The same action can be used with a nonstick frying pan. If you use a scoop, spatula, or chopsticks to stir the ingredients, remember to keep them moving. Most stir-fries should take no longer than 2–3 minutes to cook.

seasoning a wok   When you buy a wok it needs to be "seasoned" before its first use. Wash in hot soapy water to remove any packing grease or oil, then basically burn it over a high heat until the whole of the interior changes color to a deep blue, almost black appearance. Turn off the heat and smear with vegetable oil, covering all the metal, and let it soak in. After each use, you should wash and dry the wok thoroughly and rub a little oil over the surface to prevent any rusting.

a wagamama meal

The wagamama menu is designed so that one dish is enough for one person, with perhaps a side dish as well if you are hungry. We've constructed the recipes in this book for two people on the basis that two people eating together might like to share a couple of dishes. There are no hard-and-fast rules, however, and if you are catering for four people you may choose to double the quantities of one recipe and leave it at that.

japanese cooking styles   In Japan, three cooking styles are traditionally used together in the main part of the meal to ensure variety. There are seven to choose from: deep-fried (*age-mono*), grilled (*yakimono*), sautéed (*itammono*), simmered (*nimono*), steamed (*mushimono*), vinegared (*sunomono*), and dressed salads (*aemono*).

At wagamama we have rather liberally interpreted these styles so they can be incorporated in one dish. This may not be the most authentic Japanese cuisine, but we have never claimed to provide that kind of food.

This is not to say we break the rules with little thought for authenticity. In designing dishes we try to ensure balance and grounding. A monthly tasting looks at every dish being considered and, apart from tasting it, we ask lots of questions, pull it apart, and put it back together again. What we are trying to ensure is that not only does a dish taste good, but that it works both for the customer and for the kitchen preparing it. Can we do it consistently well and are there any problems? Only when we are satisfied does it go on the menu.

presentation   Presentation of the meal as well as the table setting is an integral part of Japanese dining. Both aspects are equally important in wagamama and undoubtedly enhance the enjoyment of eating noodles as well as rice dishes.

Sit in a wagamama restaurant and your table area has a paper mat and a set of wooden chopsticks specifically for you (both are disposable and produced from sustainable resources). If you find chopsticks difficult, we will give you a fork or spoon, or your server will be happy to explain how to use chopsticks. It is not difficult, but does require a little practice.

All the dishes involving liquid are served in bowls made from lacquer. Lacquer remains cool even when it contains hot liquid, so the bowl can be lifted to drink what clearly cannot be conveyed to the mouth using chopsticks. All the non-liquid-based dishes are served on plain white plates, with the ingredients cut into bite-sized pieces. So there are two issues here: how to use chopsticks and how to eat noodles.

Using chopsticks enables you to enjoy noodles in the traditional way. This involves slurping. The rationale behind this is the need to incorporate air when you eat, so that you fully sense the aroma—much more sophisticated than flavor—of the food as well as the taste. The soup is slurped and the noodles sucked and the more noise you make, the better.

spiciness   We are often asked by customers if we can spice up dishes for them. Given our streamlined restaurant service, this is not possible, which is why we leave bottles of chili sauce and soy sauce on the table so customers can help themselves. At home, however, it is possible to increase the chili heat or spiciness when you are preparing the dish. How much depends upon taste and a little experience.

We suggest that you start by following the recipes as specified; that way you know what you are dealing with. If you want more spice, for those recipes that use another sauce, such as *katsu* or *gyoza*, it is a good idea to increase slightly the amount of sauce used. Otherwise, key ingredients to pep up the spiciness include: chile, garlic, ginger, lemongrass, and *shichimi* spice. These are by no means the only ones but a 10–20 percent increase in the amount you add of these ingredients will significantly affect the final spiciness of dishes. Add slowly, taste, and experiment to get the spice kick you enjoy best.

ingredients

Listed below are those ingredients with which you may not be very familiar. Most are obtainable either in large supermarkets or ethnic food stores.

Cooked edamame.

Enoki mushrooms.

Char siu sauce   A Chinese barbecue sauce that is widely available.

Choy sum   Also known as the Chinese flowering cabbage, it has a sweet, mustardy flavor and is rich in calcium. It will keep for a few days in the fridge.

Chikuwa   Cooked Japanese fishcake, similar to *kamaboko-aka* (see right), sold by the tube in various diameters and lengths. It is available from ethnic food stores. It is mild in flavor and if you have trouble finding it, can be omitted without spoiling the overall dish.

Daikon   A mild white radish, also known as *mooli*.

Dashi   A light fish stock made from *kombu*, a seaweed (normally kelp) and dried bonito flakes (*katsuo bushi*)—although dried sardines (*niboshi*) are also used.

Dashi no moto   An instant powdered version of *dashi*, commonly used in domestic kitchens in Japan.

Edamame   Freshly steamed green soybeans. When served in the restaurants, they are lightly salted and make an ideal accompaniment to drinks. Hold to your mouth and squeeze the beans from the pod.

Enoki   These mushrooms grow in clumps and have long thin stems and well defined caps. They are delicate in flavor and if cooked correctly, retain a crunchy texture.

Fish sauce (nam pla)   A thin liquid extracted from salted, fermented fish. It should be light golden brown in color with a tangy, salty flavor. If it is dark and bitter, discard: fish sauce deteriorates once opened and darkens as it ages.

Gari, beni shoga   Pickled ginger, which was made popular with sushi and is now widely available. It is pink and both sweet and peppery in flavor and varies in strength and in the way it is cut. Fresh ginger root is also much used in Japanese cooking.

Gyoza skins   Small, round, wheat-flour skins sold in Chinese and Japanese food stores are used to make the Japanese equivalent to pot stickers (dumplings).

Kamaboko-aka   Japanese fishcakes, traditionally white with a pink outer crust, which can be bought in Oriental grocery stores.

Katsuobushi   Fermented and dried bonito fish flakes that keep forever, releasing their flavor when soaked in warm water. They are an important ingredient in *dashi* (see left).

Kombu   Kelp seaweed, sold dried (to be reconstituted in water before use) and ready-soaked.

Konnyaku   Otherwise known as black bean curd and devil's tongue, it is made from the starchy root of the *Amorphophallus konjac* plant and smells fishy. It is available from specialty Japanese food stores.

Menma   Pickled bamboo shoots which come in cans and are readily available to buy.

Mikku powder   A Japanese seasoning. You can use salt instead if you can't get *mikku*.

Mirin   Sweetened sake used for cooking.

Miso   A Japanese paste made from fermented soybeans and other ingredients. It comes in a variety of guises, from *Genmai miso*, which is made with brown rice and is chunky and rich, to sweet white *miso* which is light and delicate. Both white and yellow *miso*s are used in this book but it is worth experimenting with others to find one you particularly like. We use the red (*aka* or *sendai*) in the *miso* paste for salmon *ramen* (see page 104).

Miso soup   Made from *dashi* and flavored with *kombu* seaweed, cabbage, and dried shiitake mushrooms. It can also be made with white *miso* paste.

Noodles   In Japan there are four main types of noodles: *ramen* (Chinese style), *soba* (buckwheat and wheat noodles), *udon* (thick white wheat noodles), and *somen* (thin white noodles). Whichever type you use, noodles are always cooked in boiling unsalted water—and lots of it. They are the perfect fast food, offering a nutritionally complete meal in one bowl. A properly composed noodle soup is the quintessence of freshness and natural purity and, like pasta, is a good source of complex carbohydrates which the body can burn most easily to provide energy.

Oyster sauce   Made from oysters cooked with soy sauce and seasonings. It is brown and thick like ketchup.

Panko **bread crumbs**   These have a coarser texture than ordinary bread crumbs. They make for a much lighter and crunchier coating for deep-fried foods.

Pickled cabbage   This has a slightly sour and salty flavor and is used in small quantities and stir-fried through a dish. It is sold in cans.

Pickled ginger   See *Gari*.

Pickles   Almost every vegetable in Japan is pickled or preserved, from *daikon* to eggplant to turnip. This is generally done in salt which retains the vegetables' crunchy texture. Brands vary quite a bit and are widely available. Try several until you find one you particularly like.

Rice   Japanese rice, as it is often sold even if grown in America, is short-grained and "glutinous." This word is misleading as the rice doesn't actually contain gluten, but two kinds of starch, amylose and amylopectin (sticky rice has around 83 percent of the latter). The stickiness is important since it is eaten with chopsticks. Contrary to what might be expected, risotto or Spanish rice is closer to the Japanese variety than something like basmati, which is long-grained and not particularly 'glutinous'.

Sake   A wine made from rice. Served both warm and cold, it has similarities with dry sherry, which can be used as a substitute in recipes.

Shaoshing **wine**   Made from fermented glutinous rice, it is amber in color, about 15 percent alcohol by volume, and tastes rather sweet, reminiscent of a light sherry, which can be used as a substitute.

Shichimi **or seven-spice pepper**   A grainy mixture of chili pepper, black pepper, dried orange peel, sesame seeds, poppy seeds, slivers of *nori* seaweed, and hemp seeds. This is the perfect seasoning for *soba* and *udon* noodle dishes. It is widely available in Oriental grocery stores.

Shiitake   A variety of mushroom which, when dried, develops a strong, meaty flavor.

Spicy fish powder   A mixture of ground fried fish and *shichimi* spice (see above).

Soy sauce   Comes in two versions, light and dark. In general the light is used in cooking and is the one most commonly referred to in the recipes. Dark soy is much saltier and is used to give stronger color and flavor.

Sweet chili dipping sauce   There are various brands with the sweet/chili ratio varying. Try them all and find one you like.

Szechuan vegetables   Pickled and preserved vegetables, usually sold in cans.

Teriyaki sauce   Made from soy sauce, sake, *mirin* and ginger. It is widely available ready-made.

Tofu or bean curd   Made from soaked, mashed and strained soybeans. There are many varieties available—I recommend you use "firm" in most of these recipes. It acts like a sponge, absorbing flavors, and is an excellent protein alternative to meat.

Tsuyu **or** *tsuke* **sauce**   A traditional Japanese dipping sauce and seasoning. It is basically soy sauce flavored with seaweed (kelp), dried bonito (a type of fish), sugar, and salt. It comes in various strengths.

Wakame   A silky textured seaweed often used in soups. It is available from Oriental grocery and health food stores.

White pepper   A common seasoning ingredient in Japanese cooking.

Wakame seaweed.

Panko bread crumbs.

stocks and preparations

Good stock forms the basis of much of the food at wagamama. We use big, specially-made containers that hold vast quantities and require taps to drain off the liquid. At home you will be using a saucepan, but the principle remains the same: lots of good ingredients simmered long and slow. A stock will bubble away quite happily without much attention but there are no short-cuts if you want the real thing.

In our busy lives, however, we don't always have time to make stock from scratch. We recognize this, and give you three versions here: a domestic version of our main stock, a second stock that takes about half as long, and a third that can be prepared in minutes. All three are very different, but we are trying to achieve the best possible result within the time available. Two of them make use of chicken stock cubes; these vary quite considerably. You need to experiment to find one that suits you but, as a general rule, delicatessens and health food stores tend to stock the better examples.

Also included here are some of the basic preparations common to a number of recipes. Cooking noodles and rice, for example, and marinating meat. We also briefly cover the cutting of vegetables. Presentation is very important—in each wagamama kitchen there is a manual showing not only what the finished dish should look like, but also how to achieve it.

preparing vegetables and meat
Using chopsticks to eat means each piece of food you pick up has to be bite-sized. That need, balanced by the desire to make each dish visually appealing ensures a lot of attention is paid to the way things are chopped. The wagamama manuals show exactly how a scallion, a sweet potato, and a piece of swordfish should be cut. Perfect presentation may not be quite so critical at home, yet to the eye, a scallion or a carrot cut on the diagonal looks far more attractive than one cut on the square. As a general rule we try to avoid right angles whether slicing meat or vegetables. There is another reason, though: cutting on the diagonal means you expose a greater surface area of the ingredient to heat during stir-frying, so it cooks very fast.

Meat is marinated for two reasons: first to help tenderize it and second to impart extra flavor. The tenderizing is quite slight, and certainly won't make tough meat tender, but it does help to break down some of the enzymes. Adding flavor is the more important reason. In order to maximize the effects of the marinade, you need to "massage" it into the meat, which is best done gently by hand. Placing the meat and its marinade in a plastic bag is a good idea.

noodles   The ratio of noodles to liquid is important: in noodle soup dishes, the noodles must not only be suspended in the liquid but also form a platform on which to put the other ingredients. At wagamama we serve 4½ ounces (about 1 cup) of fresh *ramen* noodles in 2 cups of broth. We have adjusted the recipes in this book downwards slightly on the basis that most people's bowls are likely to be smaller than our *ramen* bowls.

In most of the recipes, the noodles are cooked first and then reheated in hot stock to form the finished dish. This is a real bonus which cuts down on last-minute preparation. Noodles, whatever type you buy, are very quick to cook; some only require soaking or fast boiling for 2–3 minutes (refer to the package instructions of the brand you buy). The cooking technique remains the same: as with pasta, you want plenty of boiling water and a pot big enough to accommodate the noodles and allow them to swirl around. Cooked noodles should still have some bite, or resistance—*al dente*, as the Italians say. Unlike pasta, though, it is usual to cook noodles in unsalted water, the seasoning being adjusted when you make up the final dish.

In order to stop noodles cooking you need to refresh them under lots of cold running water. The cold drained noodles will keep for a few hours in the fridge.

rice   The Japanese use short-grained rice which is cooked so it sticks together slightly—this helps when using chopsticks. You can weigh rice, but volume is often an easier and more accurate method. As a rule, if you chose not to weigh the rice, the ratio of rice to water is 2:3 and you should allow half a cup of rice per person.

Wash the rice in several changes of cold water, swirling it around with your hand to release the starch. Drain in a strainer and leave for 30 minutes. Put in a heavy pan, add the correct amount of cold water (so for 2 cups of rice, 3 cups of water), cover with a tight-fitting lid, and bring to a boil. Turn the heat down as low as it will go and cook for 10 minutes. Remove from the heat and let it sit undisturbed, lid on, for another 10 minutes. Transfer to a clean container to stop it cooking and serve.

chicken stock (1)

2¼ pounds chicken bones • 12 ounces pork bones • 1 onion, peeled and chopped • 2 carrots, chopped • 4 leeks, sliced • 1 ounce fresh ginger root, sliced • 4 Chinese (napa) cabbage leaves, roughly chopped

Put the meat bones in a large pot, cover with cold water, and bring almost to a boil. Turn the heat right down and simmer for 2 hours, skimming off any froth that rises to the surface.

Add the vegetables and another 4 cups of water, bring almost to a boil again, lower the heat, and simmer for another hour. Remove from the heat and let cool. Strain off the liquid, return to the pot and simmer for 1 hour to reduce it more. Season with the chicken stock seasoning below.

chicken stock seasoning

2 teaspoons salt • 2 teaspoons sugar • small pinch of white pepper • 1 teaspoon *dashi no moto* (see page 14)

chicken stock (2) *when you need to make stock at the same time as cooking*

2 good-quality chicken stock cubes • 4 cups uncooked chicken thighs or wings • 1 leek, finely chopped • 1 carrot, finely chopped • 4 cups water

Combine all the solid ingredients in a pot, add the water, and bring almost to boiling point, lower the heat, and simmer for 30 minutes. Strain, and proceed.

chicken stock (3) *when you want something to eat now!*

2 good-quality chicken stock cubes • 1 leek, finely chopped • 1 carrot, roughly chopped • 1-inch piece of fresh ginger root, roughly chopped • 4 cups water

Combine all the solid ingredients in a pan, cover with the water, bring to a boil, strain, and proceed.

vegetable stock (1)

4 Chinese (napa) cabbage leaves • 1 pound potatoes, peeled • 2 carrots • 2 tablespoons chopped canned tomatoes • 1 small sweet potato • $1/2$ small butternut squash • 1 white onion • 1 red onion • 1 leek • 3 quarts water

Roughly chop all the vegetables and put in a large pot with the water. Bring to a boil, then lower the heat to a gentle simmer and cook, uncovered, for 3 hours. Turn off the heat, let cool, and strain. Season with the vegetable seasoning below.

vegetable stock seasoning

2 teaspoons salt • 2 teaspoons sugar • pinch of white pepper • small pinch of *mikku* powder (see page 14)

vegetable stock (2) *when you need to make stock at the same time as cooking*

2 good-quality vegetable stock cubes • 2 Chinese (napa) cabbage leaves • 2 carrots, roughly chopped • few sprigs of flat-leaf parsley • 3 quarts water

Place all the ingredients in a large pot and bring to a boil, lower the heat, and simmer for 10–15 minutes if time, then strain.

dashi
There are two types of *dashi* fish stock, generally referred to as primary and secondary. An instant, powdered version can be bought in packets known as *dashi no moto* that simply requires water. Making *dashi* from scratch is not difficult and in Japan is considered a real test of a chef. A formal meal will start with a *dashi* broth, the quality of which determines what is likely to follow.

primary dashi

4-inch piece of *kombu* (see page 14) • handful of dried bonito flakes (*katsuobushi*, see page 14)

Lightly brush the *kombu* with a damp cloth but don't overdo it as much of the flavor lies on the surface. Put the *kombu* with 4 cups water in a large pot. Bring to a boil over medium heat. Remove from the heat, lift out the *kombu*, and reserve for use in soup. Add the bonito flakes, return the pot to the heat and bring back almost to a boil. Remove from the heat, let the bonito flakes sink to the bottom and strain. (If you leave the bonito flakes in the water for too long, they give a bitter flavor.)

secondary dashi
Proceed as above except let the *kombu* simmer gently for about 20 minutes before removing it. (This *dashi* is stronger and is traditionally used for *miso* and simmering dishes. You can reuse ingredients from primary *dashi*, or use fresh.)

vegetable dashi broth

4 cups vegetable stock • scant $1/2$ teaspoon *dashi no moto* (see page 14) • 1 teaspoon salt • 1 teaspoon sugar • pinch of *mikku* powder (see page 14) • pinch of white pepper

Heat the stock and add all the seasonings. This can be used as a broth if you or your guests don't eat fish.

curry oil

2 leeks, trimmed and finely chopped • 2 onions, trimmed and finely chopped • 1-inch piece of fresh ginger root, finely chopped • 4 garlic cloves, finely chopped • 1 cup vegetable oil • 1/2 teaspoon dried red pepper flakes • 1 bay leaf • 1 cinnamon stick • 2 star anise • 1/2 teaspoon paprika • 1 teaspoon curry powder • 1/2 teaspoon turmeric

Put all the ingredients in a large, heavy pan and cook over a low heat for 1 hour. Let cool, then strain. Covered, this will keep for a few weeks in the fridge.

miso paste

1/4 cup sake • 2 1/2 tablespoons *sendai miso* (red) • 6 1/4 tablespoons *shiro miso* (white) • 1 teaspoon sugar • 2 teaspoons sesame oil • tabasco, to taste • pinch of *shichimi* (see page 15) • generous pinch of *dashi no moto* (see page 14)

Put the sake in a small pan and bring to a boil. Light with a match, remove from the heat, and let cool. Combine the remaining ingredients in a bowl, mix well, and stir in the sake. This will keep for several days in the fridge.

coconut panko bread crumbs

4 ounces *panko* bread crumbs (see page 15) • 8 ounces dry, unsweetened coconut

Combine the bread crumbs and coconut and store in an airtight container.

shichimi spiced flour

1 cup all-purpose flour • 1 heaped teaspoon *shichimi* (see page 15) • 1 heaped teaspoon sugar • generous pinch of salt

Combine all the ingredients. Store in an airtight container until needed.

2

sauces, dips, and dressings

Ramen dishes are traditionally made up of three elements: noodles, a soup base and a prime ingredient of chicken, fish, vegetables, or meat. In reality, however, things are not quite that simple and this chapter explains why.

In addition to the three core elements, each dish needs added flavor, color, and texture. Sometimes this is achieved with a marinade, sometimes with a sauce, sometimes with a dressing. Most dishes incorporate one of these to give greater depth, an intrigue, another dimension. This is the element that leads you on, the one part of the dish that you cannot quite identify, but which provides interest.

Let's face it, noodles by themselves are quite bland, and so, too, is rice. And a good stock, while delicious, can become a little tiresome by itself. How we dress those core elements is key to building wagamama dishes and ultimately this kind of cooking is all about uniting a number of different elements to create a whole. Thus honey pork *ramen*, for example, is lent interest by the barbecue sauce used to marinate the pork; in *yasai chilli men* the chili sauce enhances the delicate flavor of the vegetables; and in *yasai itameru* it is the coconut ginger sauce that gives it oomph.

While these sauces may not form the backbone of the book, they are crucial tools. Increase the amount of ginger used in the coconut ginger sauce, or the amount of spices in the *kare lomen* sauce, and you can greatly influence the spiciness of the finished dish. It is important to remember that these recipes are designed to reflect, in a domestic environment, what we do in the restaurant. Yet as soon as you start to cook these dishes at home they become yours, and your preference may well be for something with a little more or a little less spice. It is the recipes in this chapter that will have the greatest and most immediate impact on the outcome of the finished dishes.

For those of you unfamiliar with Eastern food the presence of sugar may well be a surprise. While in the West we are attuned to the idea that sugar is bad for us, in the East it is more generally seen as another form of seasoning. There is sweetness in many foods and balancing that sweetness with acidity—or sourness—is central to the success of many dishes.

amai sauce

with vinegar, soy sauce, and ginger

Essentially a sweet and sour sauce, this is used primarily for dipping. It keeps for a few weeks in the fridge.

makes about ¹/₂ cup

1 tablespoon malt vinegar
3 tablespoons sugar
1 tablespoon light soy sauce
1 tablespoon dark soy sauce
pinch of salt
1½ tablespoons tomato ketchup
2 teaspoons tamarind paste

Gently heat the vinegar, sugar, and soy sauces in a small pan until the sugar has dissolved. Stir in the remaining ingredients and set aside to cool.

To make tamarind paste: You can buy tamarind paste in ethnic food stores, either as a concentrate that needs diluting with water, as a paste to use as is, or in a block. If you buy the block, soak for 1 hour in 2¹/₄ cups boiling water. Then manipulate the pulp with your fingers to extract as much of it as possible from the seeds and pass through a sieve, discarding what is left in the strainer.

chile and cilantro dressing

You can beef up the chile to taste, or simply sit back and enjoy the citrus flavor of the cilantro spiked with soy sauce and ginger. Use immediately before the cilantro wilts.

makes about ³/₄ cup

2 garlic cloves, peeled, chopped, and mashed with a little salt
1-inch piece of fresh ginger root, peeled and grated
1 red chile, seeded, trimmed, and finely chopped
small bunch of cilantro, roughly chopped
2 tablespoons fish sauce (*nam pla*)
3 tablespoons light soy sauce
6 tablespoons vegetable oil

Combine all the ingredients and whisk together.

Much more time is spent chopping and preparing in the kitchens than actually cooking. A whole morning can see vegetables, fish, and meat being cut for a lunchtime service, which lasts a couple of hours. In the afternoon the process is repeated all over again.

chili ramen sauce

with vinegar and nam pla

Spooned over dishes as a finishing sauce, this adds a real meaty kick, to noodles
particularly. It will keep for several weeks in the fridge.

makes about ¹/₂–²/₃ cup

2 scant teaspoons sugar

2 tablespoons malt vinegar

3 tablespoons store-bought sweet chili sauce

5 tablespoons fish sauce (*nam pla*)

Dissolve the sugar in the vinegar in a small pan over a gentle heat, let cool, and
then combine with the other ingredients.

coconut ginger sauce

with lemongrass and cilantro

Stirred into finished dishes, this sauce gives a spicy, rich finish and a flavor that is very much of the East. Take care not to overdo the coconut, it is powerful and can result in the finished dish being too rich. This will keep for about 2 days in the fridge.

makes about 2¹/₄ cups

¼ cup vegetable oil
3 garlic cloves, peeled and finely chopped
1-inch piece of fresh ginger root, peeled and grated
1-inch piece of galangal, peeled and grated
4 lemongrass stalks, outer leaves removed, finely chopped
2¼ cups hot water
½ teaspoon salt
2 teaspoons sugar
1 cup canned coconut milk
3 tablespoons roughly chopped fresh cilantro
salt and white pepper

Heat the oil in a heavy frying pan over a low heat. Add the garlic, ginger, galangal, and lemongrass. Sauté gently over medium heat for 6–8 minutes, stirring until softened and fragrant but not colored.

Add the hot water, bring to a boil then add the salt and sugar. Lower the heat and simmer for another 20 minutes until reduced by half.

Stir in the coconut milk, heat for another 2 minutes, and remove from the heat. Add the chopped cilantro. Check the seasoning before serving and adjust if necessary.

There is nothing to beat fresh coconut. It has a lively, refreshing quality that is never found in a can or carton. Yet realistically, most of us are not in a position to climb a tree or purchase the real thing every time. Can, carton, or compressed block; there is little difference between them.

cucumber dressing

with ginger and chile

This provides a good kick and a delightful crunch and I find it hard not to eat spoon-fuls as I make it. Tossed into crispy greens, it makes for an invigorating, spicy salad.

makes about 2¹/₄ cups

1 cup rice vinegar

1 cup water

¹/₂ cup sugar

1-inch piece of fresh ginger root, peeled and sliced

1 garlic clove, peeled and sliced

salt

8 ounces cucumber, grated

6 scallions, trimmed and thinly sliced

2 chiles, trimmed, seeded, and finely chopped

Put the vinegar, water, sugar, ginger, and garlic in a pan and bring to a boil. Season with salt and cook for 2 minutes, stirring until the sugar has dissolved. Let cool.

Put the cucumber and scallions in a bowl and scatter the chiles over them. Pour the cooled sauce through a strainer over the cucumber and discard the garlic and ginger. Stir well and store in the fridge for up to 7 days.

Buying the best ingredients, doing as little to them as possible and keeping what cooking time there is to a minimum is all aimed at making everything taste fresh and bright.

chili sauce

A thick, sweet red sauce spiked with chile and ginger. This sauce is used to finish dishes off and provides both color and spice. It will keep for a few days in the fridge.

makes about 1 1/4 cups

2 tablespoons vegetable oil
2 lemongrass stalks, outer leaves removed, finely chopped
1 teaspoon peeled and grated fresh ginger root
1 chile, trimmed, seeded, and finely chopped
1 red onion, peeled and finely chopped
2 garlic cloves, peeled and finely chopped
1/2 teaspoon salt
1/2 teaspoon sugar
1 tablespoon light soy sauce
1 red pepper, trimmed, seeded, and finely chopped
1 tablespoon store-bought sweet chili sauce
1 tablespoon tomato ketchup
1 1/4 cups water

Heat the vegetable oil in a small pan over a low heat until hot. Add the next eight ingredients and sauté for 7–8 minutes without coloring. Add the red pepper and continue cooking gently for 8–10 minutes. Add the remaining ingredients, bring to a boil, and simmer for 10 minutes. Blitz in a blender and use.

ebi katsu sauce
with mustard and sesame oil

A fiery finishing or dipping sauce that will keep for up to 10 days in the fridge.

makes about 1 1/4 cups

1 tablespoon English mustard powder
1 tablespoon sesame oil
1 1/4 cups store-bought sweet chili sauce
1 tablespoon tomato ketchup
1 tablespoon sugar

Blend the mustard powder and oil until smooth. Add the remaining ingredients and mix thoroughly. Transfer to a small bowl and chill until ready to use.

ebi kuzu kiri sauce

with lime juice

A sharp, intense sauce for finishing or dipping, with lots of citrus flavors balanced by the richness of the oyster sauce. This will keep for up to 10 days in the fridge.

makes about ¹/₂ cup

2 teaspoons sugar
2 tablespoons fish sauce (*nam pla*)
1 tablepoon oyster sauce
juice of 3 limes

Gently heat the sugar and fish sauce until the sugar dissolves. Let cool and combine with the oyster sauce and lime juice.

teriyaki sauce

with soy sauce and sake

Primarily used to brush grilled meats, this sauce also adds focus to finished dishes and is great for dipping. It will keep for a few weeks in the fridge. You can also buy various brands of teriyaki sauce.

makes about ¹/₂ cup

¹/₂ cup sugar
¹/₄ cup light soy sauce
2 tablespoons sake
1 teaspoon dark soy sauce

Place the sugar and light soy sauce in a small pan over a low heat and stir until the sugar has dissolved. Simmer for 5 minutes until thick, add the sake and dark soy sauce, and let cool.

barbecue sauce

By all means pour one out of a bottle, but this coating and finishing sauce really does have much more character and lick-ability. It's the kind of sauce you really don't want to finish.

makes about 1 cup

⅓ cup store-bought yellow bean sauce

⅓ cup store-bought hoisin sauce

2 teaspoons sugar

2 garlic cloves, peeled and finely minced

1 tablespoon sesame oil

pinch of white pepper

1 tablespoon dark soy sauce

2 tablespoons light soy sauce

Combine all the ingredients together. This will keep in the fridge for several days.

Bench seating means you can spread out or bunch up; couples, groups, or singles all get equal billing.

wagamama salad dressing

We have been asked for this recipe more times than any other. Until now we declined to give it out, but the pressure has proved too much!

makes about 3/4–1 cup

2 teaspoons finely chopped shallot
1-inch piece of fresh ginger root, peeled and grated
1 small garlic clove, peeled and finely chopped
1½ tablespoons rice vinegar
1 tablespoon tomato ketchup
1 tablespoon water
½ cup minus 1 tablespoon vegetable oil
3 tablespoons light soy sauce

Whisk all the ingredients together in a small bowl or screwtop jar and set aside. This can be kept in the fridge for a few days.

yaki soba dipping sauce
with soy sauce, sugar, and salt

makes about 1/2 cup

½ cup light soy sauce
2 teaspoons salt
2 teaspoons sugar
1 teaspoon dark soy sauce

Put all the ingredients in a small pan and bring to a boil. Lower the heat right down and simmer for 10 minutes. Once cool, it will keep for a few weeks in the fridge.

There is a temptation to make dressings and sauces in bulk, but after a few days some tend to lose their freshness and rather than develop their flavor, they start to level out and taste of little. Making up small quantities as and when you need them really is worth it.

Previous page: Making up the wagamama salad dressing. The essence of a good dressing lies in its simplicity; a little too much vinegar or oil and the balance is upset. Confidence is all, along with a little practice.

soy, sake, and ginger marinade

This spicy marinade also doubles as a great dipping sauce for meat, seafood, or vegetables. It will keep for up to 5 days in the fridge.

makes about 1/3–1/2 cup

3 tablespoons light soy sauce

3 tablespoons sake or dry sherry

1 tablespoon peeled and grated fresh ginger root

Combine all the ingredients in a small bowl.

gyoza sauce

with garlic, chile, and soy sauce

One of the most useful dipping sauces, all punch and attitude but with a smooth, meaty aftertaste. It will keep for several weeks in the fridge.

makes about 1 1/2 cups

1 large garlic clove, peeled and finely chopped

1 large red chile, trimmed, seeded, and finely chopped

salt

2 tablespoons sugar

1 cup minus 1 tablespoon malt vinegar

1 cup light soy sauce

1 tablespoon sesame oil

Mash the garlic and chile together with a little salt with the side of your knife to form a paste. Dissolve the sugar in the vinegar in a small pan over a low heat. Combine everything and store in a sealed container.

Most of the sauces in this chapter are essentially a way of seasoning; of adding something more; another layer. You can dip according to taste, a little or a lot depending upon preference. How much you stir into a dish can be varied depending upon how you feel. This provides variety, pace and change which means no two examples of a dish are really the same, yet the variation is subtle and controlled.

garlic herb oil
with cilantro and parsley

This is a perfect light dressing for fresh, crisp summer salads. The fresher your herbs, the longer your oil will keep.

makes about 1 cup
8 garlic cloves
few sprigs of fresh cilantro
few sprigs of fresh flat-leaf parsley
1 cup vegetable oil

Sterilize a suitable glass container by running it through the dishwasher or simmering in boiling water and then drying it on its side in a low oven—about 225°F for 30 minutes.

Put the garlic, cilantro, and parsley in the container and add the oil. Cover and store in the fridge to keep the herbs fresh. It will be ready for using in a day and should be used within 10 days.

sweet miso dressing
with sake and mirin

This is a sweet-spicy dressing, which will keep for a few days in the fridge without losing its kick.

makes about 1/2–2/3 cup
2 tablespoons *mirin* (see page 14)
2 tablespoons sake
1/4 cup sugar
1/2 cup minus 1 tablespoon yellow *miso* paste (see page 14)
1 tablespoon chili oil
1 tablespoon vegetable oil
2 teaspoons *shichimi* (see page 15)

Put the *mirin* and sake in a small pan and bring to a boil. Lower the heat, add the sugar, and stir until dissolved. Pour it onto the *miso* paste and beat until smooth. Add the oils and *shichimi* and mix thoroughly.

Both of these dressings have been designed specifically for our dishes, but they work equally well for pretty much any combination of salad ingredients from lettuce to cucumber, radishes to sweet cherry tomatoes.

tsuyu sauce

with soy sauce, mirin, and bonito

Tsuyu is a traditional Japanese dipping sauce often eaten with cold *soba* noodles. It can also be store-bought, but, homemade, it will keep for several weeks in the fridge.

makes about 1 cup

1 ¼ cups *dashi* (see page 18)
⅓ cup tea dark soy sauce
3 tablespoons *mirin* (see page 14)
½ teaspoon sugar
pinch of salt
½ ounce bonito flakes (*katsuo bushi*, see page 14)

Combine all the ingredients except the bonito flakes in a small pan and bring to the boil. Cook over a medium heat for 15 minutes until it has reduced. Remove from the heat, add the bonito flakes, and allow to soak for 1 minute. Strain, reserving the bonito for use in soup, if desired, and set aside to cool.

zasai chili sauce

with shrimp and paprika

Lots of chili, but you can tone down on the heat if you prefer things a little milder. This delicious finishing sauce will keep for a few days in the fridge.

makes about 1 cup

1 teaspoon dried chili flakes
1 red onion, chopped
2 garlic cloves, peeled and chopped
7 ounces dried shrimp
1 red pepper, trimmed, seeded, and roughly chopped
2 red chiles, trimmed, seeded, and chopped
½ teaspoon paprika
4 tablespoons vegetable oil
3 tablespoons bought sweet chili sauce
1 teaspoon sugar
½ teaspoon salt

Combine all the ingredients in a blender and blitz to a puree.

yakitori sauce

with soy, sake and mirin

A soy-based dipping and basting sauce, for fish, meat or vegetables.

makes about 1 cup

6 tablespoons sake

⅔ cup light soy sauce

6 tablespoons *mirin* **(see page 14)**

1 tablespoon caster sugar

Combine all the ingredients in a small pan and gently heat to dissolve the sugar. Set aside to cool. It will keep indefinitely in the fridge.

When lunch time happens those ramen bowls start shifting off the pass at such a rate even the staff are sometimes surprised. Speed of service is absolutely critical for us and this means in your own kitchen, dishes really do come together in minutes.

yasai vinegar

makes about 1 cup

½ cup sugar

¼ cup water

⅓ cup malt vinegar

⅓ cup light soy sauce

Dissolve the sugar in the water in a small pan over a low heat. Remove from the heat and add the remaining liquids. Cool, then bottle, and seal. The vinegar acts as a souring agent and will keep for a few weeks in the fridge.

kare lomen sauce

with lemongrass and galangal

Inspired by the flavors of Thailand, this sauce works really well with lamb (see page 130). It will keep for a few days in the fridge.

makes about ¹/₂ cup

2 lemongrass stalks, outer leaves removed, roughly chopped

1-inch piece of galangal, peeled and roughly chopped

2 garlic cloves, peeled and finely chopped

2 onions, peeled and roughly chopped

1 red pepper, trimmed, seeded, and roughly chopped

1 teaspoon sweet paprika

1 teaspoon fennel seeds

¹/₂ teaspoon chili powder

¹/₂ teaspoon turmeric

¹/₂ teaspoon curry powder

1 teaspoon shrimp paste

Combine all the ingredients in a blender and blitz to a smooth consistency.

Ginger is often given as a possible substitute for galangal, but the two are decidedly different. Galangal has a clean, almost lemony flavor, while ginger is much more soft and rounded. What they do both share however, is an elegant, spicy, peppery taste.

tori kara age sauce

with ginger, soy sauce, and sake

Ginger and soy sauce are such a winning combination it is hard not to drizzle this sauce over everything from plain rice and noodles to *gyozas*. It also makes a great marinade for chicken. And the good thing is it will keep indefinitely in the fridge, so you can make lots and have it on hand whenever you need it.

makes about 3 cups
1-inch piece of fresh ginger root, peeled and grated
3 cups light soy sauce
¼ cup sake
1 teaspoon sugar
1 tablespoon oyster sauce

Combine all the ingredients in a pan and heat gently to dissolve the sugar. Set aside to cool.

yasai soba dressing

with lemongrass and ginger

This is a thick dressing, designed to coat noodles rather than salad greens, although the latter are rather good too. It will keep for months in the fridge.

makes about ²/₃ cup
²/₃ cup teriyaki sauce, homemade (see page 28) or store-bought
4½ tablespoons crushed yellow bean sauce
1 lemongrass stalk, outer leaves removed, finely sliced
1 tablespoon peeled and grated fresh ginger root

Put all the ingredients in a mixing bowl and combine until blended.

3

sides and other small dishes

Eating at wagamama is very informal. Food arrives as it is cooked, making it as fresh and hot as possible. We eschew the traditional structure of appetizers and main courses in favor of a more accessible route. If you'd like a second plate of *gyozas*, it is simple to order and is likely to be delivered in moments. If you are joined by later-comers, they are easily accommodated.

The reasons for this approach are many, but chief among them is the more Oriental way of structuring a meal. Several dishes appear on the table at once. The idea is to be as relaxed and easy-going as possible. And the sharing aspect is integral.

As a result of this approach "sides" is about as far as it goes in terms of first courses. Sides are really things to nibble on while you sip a glass of cold beer, white wine, or a juice, or may provide an extra offering for people who are particularly hungry. This chapter is devoted to those dishes that are perfect to serve before your main course, or to accompany a range of other dishes.

We have gained something of a reputation for our *gyozas*: small dumplings filled with combinations of meat, fish, and vegetables, and presented with various dipping sauces that typically feature a little chili, ginger perhaps, and maybe soy sauce. Most of these sauces will keep for a few days if not weeks in the fridge, so there is no need to make them fresh every time. *Gyozas* can be deep-fried, grilled, or steamed. We do them all three ways on the menu for variety, but for cooking at home we'd suggest you find the style you like best and stick with that.

Several recipes feature chicken thigh meat. Ground chicken is not the same thing at all as it tends not to include the brown thigh meat. The best option is to buy thighs and then skin and bone them, and chop them into cubes or blitz briefly in a food processor.

Most of the sides featured here are morsels to be picked up using chopsticks or fingers, but there are a few more substantial dishes as well. The oven-steamed mussels in sake and ginger (see page 55), for example, is a somewhat larger serving but the idea remains the same: something to eat with the fingers in a relaxed and informal way. A few of the recipes for sides, such as the *gyozas*, are designed for serving more than two people as it is often just not practical to break down the amounts you'd need for such a small number.

The *ebi katsu* (bread-crumbed and shallow-fried shrimp, see page 52) are very typical of the bar snacks found around Tokyo, indeed throughout Japan. They are often served alongside *edamame* (soybeans in the pod), which is one of our most popular dishes, the ultimate nibble food and a far cry from peanuts. You may need to go to a specialty store to find them, but very little is needed to turn them into an excellent snack (see page 46).

negima yakitori

char-broiled chicken with yakitori sauce

One of our most popular sides. Perfect with an ice-cold beer, the *yakitori* sauce adds a subtle spiciness. A really simple and easy appetizer.

10 ounces boneless, skinless chicken thigh meat (see page 41)
12 scallions
salt and white pepper
2 tablespoons vegetable oil
¼ cup *yakitori* sauce (see page 37)
6 bamboo skewers, soaked in cold water for 2 hours

Cut the chicken into 1-inch cubes. Trim the green end and root of the scallion and cut into 1-inch pieces from the root up. Thread the chicken and scallion pieces alternately onto the skewers (each skewer should have 3 pieces of chicken and 2 pieces of scallion). Season with salt and white pepper.

Heat a heavy frying pan or grill pan over medium heat for 1–2 minutes or until hot and almost smoking and add the oil. Cook the skewers, turning frequently, for about 5–6 minutes until golden brown. Drain on paper towels to remove any excess oil and brush with the *yakitori* sauce. Serve immediately.

Talking about the menu and the food: some customers order by number, others less familiar with the menu like to have things explained. There is no formality or structure at wagamama, you order as you like and the food comes as soon as it is ready.

caramelized sweet potatoes
with golden syrup and black sesame seeds

9 ounces sweet potato, peeled and cut into thin wedges
vegetable oil, for deep-frying
1 teaspoon golden syrup
juice of ½ lemon
1 teaspoon black sesame seeds, for sprinkling

Soak the sweet potato wedges for 5 minutes in cold water. Drain well, then pat dry with paper towels.

Fill a large pan one-third full of oil and heat to 350°F or until a cube of bread added to the oil browns in 30 seconds. Carefully lower the wedges into the hot oil and cook for 5 minutes or until golden brown. Remove from the oil and drain well on paper towels.

Combine the syrup with the lemon juice and heat in a small saucepan. Pour it over the potato wedges, stir well to coat, then transfer to a serving plate and sprinkle with the sesame seeds.

edamame

steamed soybeans with chile

This recipe is from our restaurants in Sydney where they like things a touch more spicy. In the UK, we don't use the oil or the chile and simply steam the beans for 2 minutes, then add salt. Why not try both versions—either way, the dish is surprisingly addictive and makes a great appetizer.

8 ounces *edamame* in their pods
1 red chile, trimmed, seeded, and finely chopped
1 teaspoon sesame oil
1 teaspoon salt

Put the *edamame* in a steamer over a pan of salted water and cook for 1–2 minutes, until firm but still with a bite. Drain thoroughly.

Heat a frying pan until hot and add the chile and sesame oil. Add the *edamame* and stir-fry for 1 minute. Serve, sprinkled with salt, in a bowl and provide another bowl for the pods.

miso soup and pickles

with scallions and wakame

1 tablespoon dried *wakame* (see page 15), soaked in cold water for 5 minutes
2¼ cups *dashi*, made with *dashi no moto* (see page 14) according to
   the package instructions
3 tablespoons *miso* paste (see page 19)
pinch of *mikku* powder (see page 14)
2 scallions, trimmed and sliced
pickles (see page 15), for serving

Drain the soaked *wakame* and roughly chop. Bring the *dashi* to a boil and whisk in the *miso* paste. Add the *mikku* powder.

Divide the *wakame* and scallions between 2 cups or small bowls and pour the *miso* soup over them. Serve with a portion (1 scant tablespoonful per person) of mixed pickles.

dashi is a stock based on fish and seaweed. It is key to Japanese cooking and a chef is traditionally judged on its quality. Its simplicity is telling. *Miso* soup is a combination of *dashi* flavored with *miso*, in our case white *miso* but there are other versions. We also add *wakame* (seaweed) and scallion. The pickles are traditional and while refrigeration has made the need for pickling largely redundant, in Japan the taste for these crunchy morsels is as strong as ever.

raw salad

mixed greens with red pepper, cherry tomatoes, and wagamama dressing

½ red pepper, trimmed, seeded, and finely sliced
4 handfuls of various salad greens
¼ cup wagamama salad dressing (see page 32)
salt and white pepper
6 cherry tomatoes, left whole or cut in half
6 slices of cucumber

Plunge the pepper slices into iced water until they curl, which will take a few minutes.

   Combine the salad greens with the dressing in a bowl and toss well. Check the seasoning. Divide the greens between 2 plates and scatter the tomatoes, cucumber, and red pepper over them.

yasai yakitori

grilled vegetable skewers with yakitori sauce

1 zucchini, cut into 1-inch slices

3 thick scallions, bulb end only, cut into 1-inch chunks

1 orange pepper, trimmed, seeded, and cut into 1-inch chunks

6 button mushrooms

6 cherry tomatoes

2 tablespoons vegetable oil

salt and white pepper

2 tablespoons *yakitori* sauce (see page 37)

6 bamboo skewers, soaked in cold water for 2 hours

Thread 1 piece of vegetable per skewer so each skewer contains 5 pieces. Brush each skewer lightly with vegetable oil and season with salt and white pepper.

Heat a heavy frying pan or grill pan over medium heat for 1–2 minutes until hot and almost smoking. Cook the skewers, turning frequently, for 4–5 minutes until golden brown.

Drain on paper towels to remove excess oil. Brush with the *yakitori* sauce and serve immediately.

yasai gyoza

steamed vegetable dumplings with soy sauce and sesame oil

Easy to prepare, quick to cook, but you need to make about 30 as it is very hard to get the mixture the correct consistency for less. If you are catering for smaller numbers, they will freeze well.

makes about 30

9 ounces canned water chestnuts, drained
2 ounces green cabbage
½ ounce Chinese cabbage (napa cabbage)
1 small carrot
½ onion
1 celery stalk
¼ cup cornstarch
1 tablespoon light soy sauce
1 tablespoon sesame oil
1 teaspoon salt
½ teaspoon sugar
pinch of white pepper
1 package *gyoza* skins (see page 14)
vegetable oil, for frying
gyoza sauce, for serving (see page 33)

Put the water chestnuts, cabbage, Chinese cabbage, carrot, onion and celery in a food processor and pulse briefly until finely chopped. (Do not over-blend or the mixture will become a pulp.) Using a clean lintfree dishtowel, gently but firmly squeeze the mixture to remove the excess moisture. Tip into a large bowl and stir in the cornstarch, soy sauce, sesame oil, salt, sugar, and white pepper.

Put a teaspoonful of the mixture in the center of each *gyoza* skin. Moisten one of the edges with a little water, then fold it over to create a half-moon shape. Press down, to form a neat crescent.

Heat a large frying pan over medium heat for 1–2 minutes or until hot and almost smoking and add 1 tablespoon of vegetable oil. Put 3 or 4 of the dumplings in the pan and sauté gently for 2 minutes over a low heat until just starting to brown. Don't be tempted to overcrowd the pan or they will stew.

Remove the pan from the heat, add 3 tablespoons of water, and cover immediately with a lid or with aluminum foil. Return to the heat for 1 minute, then remove and set aside for another 2 minutes, by which time the *gyozas* will be heated through. Repeat for the remaining *gyozas*.

Perfect finger food, gyozas are often shared in the restaurants and make great party food. We serve them with a chili, garlic, and soy sauce dip.

ebi gyoza

shrimp, soy sauce, and sesame dumplings

makes about 30

5 ounces cooked peeled shrimp

4½ ounces canned water chestnuts, drained

2 scallions, trimmed

4 ounces fresh baby spinach leaves

1 tablespoon cornstarch

pinch each of salt, sugar, and white pepper

1 teaspoon oyster sauce

1 teaspoon light soy sauce

1 teaspoon sesame oil

1 package *gyoza* skins (see page 14)

vegetable oil, for frying

gyoza sauce, for serving (see page 33)

Gyozas are really easy and fun to make, the secret is not to over-blend the filling and to make sure you don't over-fill the skin. Practice makes perfect, as they say.

Put the shrimp, water chestnuts, and scallions in a food processor and blitz until finely minced.

Put the spinach in a colander over the sink and wilt by pouring a kettle of boiling water over it. Let cool and drain, then squeeze gently but firmly to remove the excess water.

Finely chop the spinach and stir into the shrimp mixture along with the cornstarch, salt, sugar, white pepper, oyster sauce, soy sauce, and sesame oil.

Put a teaspoonful of the mixture in the center of each *gyoza* skin. Moisten one of the edges with a little water, then fold it over to create a half-moon shape. Press down, to form a neat crescent.

Heat a large frying pan over medium heat for 1–2 minutes or until hot and almost smoking and add 1 tablespoon of vegetable oil. Put 3 or 4 of the dumplings in the pan and sauté gently for 2 minutes over a low heat until just starting to brown. Don't be tempted to overcrowd the pan or they will stew.

Remove the pan from the heat, add 3 tablespoons of water, and cover immediately with a lid or with aluminum foil. Return to the heat for 1 minute, then remove and set aside for another 2 minutes, by which time the *gyozas* will be heated through. Repeat for the remaining *gyozas*.

ebi katsu

pan-fried tiger shrimp with chili and garlic dipping sauce

Nobody does bread crumbs better than the Japanese. They have several grades and the top grade costs serious money. It's all in the texture, crispy but not too heavy. And remember to use a fresh and pure vegetable oil for frying, you want as neutral a flavor as possible.

1 heaped tablespoon flour, seasoned with a pinch of salt
1 egg, beaten
1 ounce *panko* bread crumbs (see page 15)
10 raw tiger shrimp, peeled and deveined, tail left on
¼ cup vegetable oil
2 tablespoons *ebi katsu* sauce (see page 27)
1 lime, cut in half, for serving

Put the flour, beaten egg, and bread crumbs into three separate bowls. Dip each shrimp first in the flour, then the egg, and finally the crumbs. Put on a clean plate lined with paper towels and press the crumbs onto the shrimp to stop them from falling off. Chill until ready to use.

Heat a heavy frying pan over medium heat for 1–2 minutes or until hot and almost smoking and add the vegetable oil. Pan-fry the shrimp in 2 batches, so as not to overcrowd the frying pan, until golden brown on both sides.

Arrange on a plate with a small bowl of the *ebi katsu* sauce and lime halves.

" *Customers often find pronouncing the names of the dishes difficult. We all do. It doesn't matter a bit and that makes me smile.* "
Una, Dublin

cured marinated salmon salad

with chile, lime juice, and cucumber

The "team" part of the T-shirt logo is central to the wagamama management philosophy of kaizen: everyone concerned with wagamama is actively involved in suggesting and implementing small improvements to the operation.

1 teaspoon sugar

juice of 1 lime, plus 2 tablespoons

1 garlic clove, peeled, finely chopped, and mashed with a little salt

1 tablespoon sesame oil

3 tablespoons light soy sauce

2 slices (3 ounces) fresh salmon, cut into 2mm (1/8-inch) strips

5 ounces bean sprouts

3 ounces cucumber, grated

1–2 red chiles, trimmed and very thinly sliced on the diagonal

2 sprigs of flat-leaf parsley, finely chopped

To make the marinade, combine the sugar and 2 tablespoons of the lime juice in a small bowl and stir until the sugar has dissolved. Add the garlic, sesame oil, and soy sauce, and stir until emulsified.

Toss the salmon strips in 4 tablespoons of the marinade. Cover and place in the fridge for 3 hours.

To serve, arrange the salmon strips in a flower pattern on 2 plates, working from the outside edge of the plate inwards. Pour the remaining marinade around the plate edge.

Blanch the bean sprouts in boiling water for 10 seconds, drain, and refresh under cold running water. Shake off the excess water and combine with the cucumber and chile. Sprinkle with the juice of the whole lime. Pile into the center of each plate and scatter the parsley over it.

oven-steamed mussels

in sake, soy sauce, and ginger

1 pound, 2 ounces live mussels

2 leeks, trimmed and julienned

1 red onion, peeled and thinly sliced

1 carrot, peeled and julienned

4 scallions, trimmed and julienned

1 green chile, trimmed and thinly sliced

2 garlic cloves, peeled and crushed

1 tablespoon fresh ginger root, peeled and julienned

¼ cup sake

2 tablespoons light soy sauce

2 tablespoons butter

2 pieces of turkey foil, each 24 inches square

Preheat the oven to 400°F. Clean and debeard the mussels. Tap any open ones and discard any that do not close. Lay out the squares of foil, shiny side up.

Mix together the mussels and all the vegetables, along with the chile, garlic, and ginger in a large bowl. Divide the mixture into 2, put in the center of each square ,and pull up the edges to begin to form a bundle.

Pour the sake and soy sauce over them and dot with the butter. Scrunch up the foil edges to form a tightly closed bundle. Put on 2 baking sheets and cook in the oven for 15 minutes or until the mussel shells have opened. Tip into bowls to serve.

Although we don't serve mussels in the restaurants, these inexpensive delicacies are perfect for flavoring with the likes of ginger, sake, and soy sauce. A more dramatic way of serving them is to present them in the foil, and once opened, the steam engulfs you with a heady mixture of ginger and soy.

chicken gyoza

chicken, cabbage, and chive dumplings with oyster sauce

To say we sell lots of *gyozas* in the restaurants is a bit of an understatement, every-one seems to adore them whether stuffed with shrimp, duck, chicken, or vegetables.

makes about 30

4 ounces Chinese cabbage (napa cabbage)

5 ounces green cabbage

3½ ounces canned water chestnuts, drained

9 ounces boneless, skinless chicken thigh meat, ground (see page 41)

1 ounce fresh chives, finely chopped

¼ cup cornflour

1 teaspoon sesame oil

1 tablespoon oyster sauce

1 tablespoon light soy sauce

1 teaspoon sugar

pinch of salt and white pepper

1 package *gyoza* skins (see page 14)

vegetable oil, for frying

gyoza sauce, for serving (see page 33)

Put the Chinese cabbage, green cabbage, and water chestnuts in a food processor and pulse until finely chopped but not pureed. Using a clean lintfree dishtowel, squeeze the mixture gently but firmly to remove the excess moisture, then tip into a bowl and add the ground chicken, chives, cornstarch, sesame oil, oyster sauce, soy sauce, sugar, salt, and white pepper.

Put a teaspoonful of the mixture in the center of each *gyoza* skin. Moisten one of the edges with a little water, then fold it over to create a half-moon shape. Press down, to form a neat crescent.

Heat a large frying pan over medium heat for 1–2 minutes or until hot and almost smoking and add 1 tablespoon of vegetable oil. Put 3 or 4 of the dumplings in the pan and sauté gently for 2 minutes over a low heat until just starting to brown. Don't be tempted to overcrowd the pan or they will stew.

Remove the pan from the heat, add 3 tablespoons of water, and cover immedi-ately with a lid or with aluminum foil. Return to the heat for 1 minute, then remove and set aside for another 2 minutes, by which time the *gyozas* will be heated through. Repeat for the remaining *gyozas*.

spiced tofu katsu

crispy tofu with sweet chili sauce

Enticingly spicy with crispy bread crumbs and soft, creamy tofu underneath; deep-frying is only one of the many ways to cook this versatile ingredient. Tofu (or bean curd), the milk of soybeans, is rich in protein and virtually tasteless, but it works by absorbing all sorts of exciting flavors. It is by no means a modern food and is held in such high regard, some countries refer to it as the "meat of the fields."

10 ounces firm tofu, cut into 4 equal-sized rectangles, about ½-inch thick
1 tablespoon *shichimi* (see page 15)
1 teaspoon salt
3 tablespoons all-purpose flour
2 eggs, beaten
2 ounces *panko* bread crumbs (see page 15)
vegetable oil, for deep-frying
¼ cup store-bought sweet chili sauce, for dipping

Pat the tofu cubes dry with paper towels to remove the excess water. In a small bowl, mix together the *shichimi,* salt, and flour. Put the beaten egg in another bowl and the bread crumbs in a third. Dip the tofu slices first in the spiced flour, then in the beaten egg, and finally in the bread crumbs. Dip them again in the egg and the breadcrumbs for a really good coating.

Fill a large pan one-third full with oil and heat until 350°F or until a cube of bread added to the oil browns in 30 seconds. Deep-fry the coated tofu until golden brown. Drain on paper towels. Put onto 2 plates, with a small dish of sweet chili sauce.

tori kara age

deep-fried chicken with soy sauce and sake

10 ounces boneless, skinless chicken thigh meat, cut into 1-inch
  cubes (see page 41)

3 tablespoons *tori kara age* sauce (see page 39)

1 egg, beaten

½ teaspoon dried thyme

½ teaspoon dried oregano

2 teaspoons cornstarch

vegetable oil, for deep frying

for serving

2 tablespoons *gyoza* sauce (see page 33)

1 lime, cut into wedges

Marinate the chicken in a shallow bowl in the *tori kara age* sauce for at least 1 hour
and if possible, overnight.

In another bowl, mix together the egg, herbs, and cornstarch until smooth, then
add the marinated chicken pieces and turn to coat thoroughly.

Fill a large pan one-third full with vegetable oil and heat to 350°F or until a
cube of bread added to the oil browns in 30 seconds. Deep-fry the chicken for
5 minutes until golden brown, using a pair of chopsticks or tongs to separate any
cubes that stick together.

Drain on paper towels. Serve with a small dish of *gyoza* sauce and a wedge
of lime.

*We have limited the
number of deep-fried
recipes in this book, but
this chicken is too good
to miss out on, crispy
and succulent with a
gentle spicy kick. Finger
food to linger over.*

seared beef sashimi

beef carpaccio and vegetable salad with ginger and cilantro

A dish that provides amazing colour as well as taste. In the Sydney restaurants we serve this with *gyoza* sauce (see page 33), which makes a delicious dip.

4 ounces tenderloin steak

salt and white pepper

1 small carrot, peeled and very thinly sliced lengthwise

½ English cucumber, seeded and thinly sliced lengthwise

4 scallions, trimmed and thinly sliced

1 ounce snow peas, thinly sliced lengthwise

½ red onion, peeled and thinly sliced

½ green chile, trimmed, seeded, and thinly sliced lengthwise

½ red chile, trimmed, seeded, and thinly sliced lengthwise

½ tablespoon fresh ginger root, peeled, and julienned

1 ½ tablespoons olive oil, for drizzling

1 ½ tablespoons light soy sauce, for drizzling

4 sprigs of cilantro (coriander leaves), for garnishing

Season the steak with salt and pepper. Heat a nonstick frying pan until really hot and almost smoking and sear the beef for 15 seconds on each side until golden brown.

Remove the beef from the heat and plunge it into iced water for about 30 seconds. Wrap in plastic wrap and place in the freezer for 1 hour to firm up.

Put all the vegetables, chiles, and ginger into fresh iced water for 30 minutes to crisp. Remove and drain thoroughly.

To serve, slice the beef into wafer-thin slices and arrange around the edge of a serving plate. Put the vegetable mixture in the center.

Drizzle the olive oil over the steak and vegetables, followed by the soy sauce, and top with the cilantro.

4
chicken

I'm walking down a shopping mall in the center of Tokyo feeling a little hungry. Past the boutiques and electronic shops I'm suddenly hit by the aroma of grilling chicken. The bar is doing a roaring trade in ice-cold beers and the chef is skillfully flipping skewers of chicken on his long chargrill. Time for a break.

Grilled chicken, roast chicken, even poached chicken is hard to resist, one of those smells that we all associate with comfort and warmth. *Negima yakitori* (see page 42) is one of the most popular sides at wagamama, and chicken features widely on the menu because of its universal popularity.

The Japanese are not traditionally big meat eaters—lack of land is one of the practical reasons for this, but religion and tradition also play their part. Both chicken and duck are popular, not least because the meat cooks quickly. In dishes like chicken chili *men* and *yaki soba,* the speed of cooking means chicken is ideal as a protein element kept in balance with all the other ingredients.

Chicken is widely used in all Asian cooking, its ability to partner ingredients—chile and other spices, sauces, and marinades—making it a fantastic all-rounder. Often it is combined with shrimp, an Eastern surf 'n' turf experience that brings a freshness and vitality; our signature dish, wagamama *ramen*, a light, aromatic broth with noodles, chicken, shrimp, and crabsticks combined with vegetables, is a case in point. A meal in a bowl and very much the way of the noodle.

When buying chicken, seek out free-range and, if possible, organic birds. The extra cost should be reflected in the eating; a fuller, more rounded flavor and a firm texture. Chickens are among the most intensively farmed animals and some examples taste of little and come with a decidedly pappy texture. Alternatives include guinea fowl (slightly gamier in flavor and with a firmer flesh) and quail.

The same rules on shopping apply to duck, although the less good examples tend to be very tough and fatty. Seek out a decent supplier and stick to them.

Portion packs offer convenience, but at a price. A whole bird is not difficult to cut up and judicious use of the freezer will give you two meals for two people from one bird and a carcass for making stock. While breast meat is often heralded as being superior, both leg and thigh meat is often more moist and tends to deliver more flavor (see page 41).

When marinating chicken, you need to toss the meat gently in your chosen marinade so it combines. This is best done with your hands or, failing that, use a couple of wooden spoons so the flesh isn't bruised. For the restaurants, chicken is marinated and then sealed in bags to allow the flavors to develop. This technique works well at home too, and ensures efficient use of fridge space.

chicken tama rice

charbroiled chicken with oyster sauce and stir-fried vegetables

1 cup Japanese or other short-grain rice

2 boneless, skinless chicken breasts

vegetable oil, for frying

salt and white pepper

2 garlic cloves, crushed

1 teaspoon fresh ginger root, grated

1 large zucchini, sliced

15 *poku* mushrooms, sliced ¼-inch thick

2 tablespoons *shaoshing* wine (see page 15)

⅔ cup water

1 teaspoon sugar

2 tablespoons oyster sauce

½ teaspoon cornstarch

1 egg, beaten

2 teaspoons sesame oil

Cook the rice in a large pan of boiling water until tender. Drain and set aside.

Preheat the broiler or grill pan. Lightly oil the chicken breasts with vegetable oil, season and broil or grill for 4 minutes on each side, or until cooked through. Let rest for 5 minutes, slice on the diagonal, and set aside.

Heat a wok over medium heat for 1–2 minutes or until completely hot and almost smoking and add 3 tablespoons of vegetable oil. Add the garlic and ginger and stir-fry for 10 seconds. Add the zucchini and mushrooms and stir-fry for 1 minute. Pour in the wine and water, then bring to a boil. Add ½ teaspoon salt, the sugar, and oyster sauce.

Make a paste with the cornstarch and a little cold water. Then skim off 2 tablespoons of the liquid in the wok, mix with the cornstarch paste, return to the wok, and bring back to a boil. Add the egg to the sauce and cook until soft but don't let it curdle. Stir the sesame oil through it.

Divide the rice between 2 plates, place the charbroiled chicken breast on top, and pour the sauce over it.

chicken chili men

stir-fried chicken with green pepper, scallions, and noodles

10 ounces *soba* noodles

3 tablespoons vegetable oil

2 boneless, skinless chicken breasts, cut on the diagonal into ½-inch strips

1 green pepper, trimmed, seeded, and thinly sliced

1 small zucchini, thinly sliced

½ red onion, peeled and thinly sliced

4 scallions, trimmed and cut into 1-inch lengths

1¼ cups chili sauce (see page 27)

Cook the noodles in a large pot of boiling water for 2–3 minutes or until just tender. Drain thoroughly and refresh under cold water.

Heat a wok over medium heat for 1–2 minutes or until completely hot and almost smoking and add the vegetable oil. Add the chicken, pepper, zucchini, red onion, and scallions, and stir-fry for 3–4 minutes until the chicken is cooked and the vegetables are lightly colored. Add the chili sauce and bring to a boil. Divide the noodles between 2 bowls and top with the stir-fry.

cha han

stir-fried chicken and shrimp with corn, mushrooms, and fragrant rice

7 ounces boneless, skinless chicken thigh meat (see page 41)

2 tablespoons *yakitori* sauce (see page 37)

2 tablespoons vegetable oil

8 cooked, peeled shrimp

2 tablespoons canned corn, well drained

2 tablespoons snow peas, finely sliced

4 button mushrooms, finely sliced

2 scallions, trimmed and cut into 1-inch lengths

2 eggs, beaten

3 ounces cooked Thai fragrant rice

salt

2 tablespoons light soy sauce

miso soup and pickles (see page 46), for serving

Combine the chicken and the *yakitori* sauce in a bowl. Work gently with your fingers for a few minutes, turning the meat in the sauce. Marinate for at least 30 minutes (1 hour is even better). Remove the chicken, reserving the marinade, and cut the meat on the diagonal into thin slices.

Heat a wok over medium heat for 1–2 minutes or until completely hot and almost smoking and add the vegetable oil. Add the shrimp, corn, snow peas, mushrooms, and scallions, along with the chicken and stir-fry over medium heat for about 5 minutes until the vegetables just start to wilt and the chicken is cooked. Add the egg and continue to stir-fry until it is just scrambled.

Add the rice. Season with salt and soy sauce and continue stir-frying until everything is mixed evenly and the rice heated through. Divide between 2 bowls and serve with *miso* soup and pickles.

cha han is easily one of the most popular dishes on the menu. With lots of vegetables, its light seasoning of *yakitori* sauce, and ever-popular chicken and shrimp, the combination seems to be a winner with young and old alike —my son says it's definitely his favorite. All the preparation for this dish happens up-front. Cooking is really a matter of minutes and the whole assembly can be on the table in less than 20.

chicken ramen

charbroiled chicken and noodle soup with bok choy and bamboo

Combine noodles, hot stock, fresh vegetables, and lightly broiled chicken, and you have a complete meal in a bowl. Fast food really doesn't get better than this.

2 boneless, skinless chicken breasts

vegetable oil, for oiling

salt and white pepper

9 ounces *ramen* noodles

4 cups chicken or vegetable stock (see pages 17 and 18)

2 bok choy, trimmed and roughly chopped (or 2 handfuls of baby spinach leaves)

12 pieces *menma* (canned bamboo shoots), drained

4 scallions, trimmed and finely sliced

Preheat the broiler or grill. Lightly oil and season the chicken breasts and broil or grill for 4 minutes on each side, or until cooked through. Let rest for 5 minutes, slice on the diagonal, and set aside.

Cook the noodles in a large pot of boiling water for 2–3 minutes until just tender. Drain, refresh under cold running water, and divide between 2 bowls.

Heat the chicken or vegetable stock until boiling. Put the bok choy on top of the noodles and ladle in the stock. Top with the sliced chicken, *menma*, and scallions.

Thank you. I am a devoted fan. Could you please send me the recipe for chicken ramen. I could eat it forever!
Trey, USA

ginger chicken teppan

stir-fried chicken and noodles with chile, cilantro, and ginger

7 ounces *udon* noodles

handful of snow peas, finely sliced

½ red onion, peeled and thickly sliced

4 scallions, trimmed and cut into 1-inch lengths

1 garlic clove, peeled and finely sliced

1 tablespoon fresh ginger root, peeled and grated

2 tablespoons roughly chopped cilantro (coriander leaves)

1 red chile, seeded and finely sliced

2 handfuls of bean sprouts

3 tablespoons *tsuyu* sauce (see page 36)

2 eggs, beaten

2 tablespoons vegetable oil

10½ ounces boneless, skinless chicken thigh meat, cut into strips

2 teaspoons pickled ginger *(gari*, see page 14*)*, for scattering

6 sprigs of cilantro, for garnishing

Cook the noodles in a large pot of boiling water for 2–3 minutes or until just tender. Drain and refresh under cold running water. Put all the ingredients except the oil, chicken, pickled ginger, and cilantro sprigs in a large bowl, adding in the noodles last, and mix to combine.

Heat a wok over medium heat for 1–2 minutes or until completely hot and almost smoking and add the vegetable oil. Add the chicken and stir-fry for 5 minutes, or until cooked. Add everything from the bowl and stir-fry for 3–4 minutes. Check the seasoning, then divide the stir-fry between 2 plates and scatter the pickled ginger and cilantro sprigs on top.

Bean sprouts may not major on the flavor front, but their crunchy texture is a key aspect in many stir-fry dishes and salads.

When it comes to "the way of the noodle" the idea is to make slurping noises while eating—the extra oxygen enhances the flavour of the dish. The truth is it is very difficult to eat noodles with chopsticks and not slurp. Napkins are to be advised and reducing the distance from bowl to mouth also helps. In Japan, the bowl is often held up close to the face and is the reason why the bowls are not made from china—they would simply get too hot.

chicken and shrimp hot pot

with tofu, mushrooms, and soy sauce

This recipe is a real reviver—soothing, comforting, and gentle. A reminder of how very subtle and delicate Japanese food can be.

2½ cups *dashi*, made with *dashi no moto* (see page 14) according to
   package instructions
2 tablespoons sake
1 tablespoon light soy sauce
pinch of salt
2 teaspoons *mirin* (see page 14)
8 ounces boneless, skinless chicken thigh meat, cut into 1-inch cubes
4 shiitake mushrooms, roughly chopped
2 Chinese cabbage (napa cabbage) leaves, cut into 1-inch-wide strips
4 scallions, trimmed and cut into ¾-inch lengths
5 x 1-inch cubes firm tofu
9 ounces white *ramen* noodles
small bunch of Chinese chives
4 cooked tiger shrimp, unpeeled

Put the *dashi,* sake, soy sauce, salt, and *mirin* in a pan and bring to a boil. Add the chicken, cover, and lower the heat. Simmer for 3 minutes until the chicken is almost cooked through. Add the remaining ingredients, except for the shrimp, and cook for another 2–3 minutes. Remove from the heat, add the shrimp, and set aside for 2 minutes to heat the shrimp through. Divide between 2 bowls.

Central to wagamama is the idea of a long kitchen and bench seating which is perpendicular to it. It means food can be delivered quickly without any fuss. This broke away from the traditional concept of a restaurant kitchen and dining room being separate elements—the constant noise and buzz of the kitchen is all part of the wagamama experience.

teriyaki chicken stir-fry

with chile, garlic, scallion, and rice

9 ounces boneless, skinless chicken breast or thigh meat (see page 41),
   sliced into ½-inch strips
1 red chile, trimmed and finely sliced
1 teaspoon garlic paste (homemade or store-bought)
¼ cup teriyaki sauce, homemade (see page 28) or store-bought
2 tablespoons vegetable oil
4 ounces bean sprouts
½ red onion, peeled and thickly sliced
½ red pepper, trimmed, seeded, and cut into strips
3 ounces bok choy, cut in half
pinch of salt
pinch of sugar
1 scallion, trimmed and finely sliced on the diagonal, for garnishing
cooked plain boiled rice, for serving

Place the chicken, chile, garlic paste, and teriyaki sauce in a large bowl or clean plastic bag and mix thoroughly. Cover and marinate in the fridge for 2–3 hours.

Heat a wok over medium heat for 1–2 minutes or until completely hot and almost smoking and add the oil. Add the chicken and any marinade from the bowl, and stir-fry for about 5 minutes until all the meat is golden. Continue cooking for another minute, then add the bean sprouts, red onion, red pepper, and bok choy.

Stir-fry for another 2 minutes, ensuring the bottom of the wok doesn't burn (you can add a teaspoon of water during this time to take some of the heat out of the wok). Season to taste with salt and sugar. Divide between 2 plates, top with scallion slices, and serve with the rice.

positive eating and living drives the menu and defines what wagamama is all about. Wagamama means wilfulness or self-ishness: selfishness in terms of looking after oneself, looking after oneself in terms of positive eating and positive living. Before wagamama, fast food implied a compromise. The idea of providing well-cooked, well-presented nutritious meals prepared to order in comfortable surroundings had never been achieved on this scale before.

yaki udon

stir-fried chicken with shiitake mushrooms, leek, and red pepper

7 ounces boneless, skinless chicken thigh meat (see page 41)

2 tablespoons *yakitori* sauce (see page 37)

7 ounces *udon* noodles

1 egg

2 tablespoons *yaki soba* sauce (see page 32)

2 tablespoons curry oil (see page 19)

4 shiitake mushrooms, sliced

3 ounces leeks, finely chopped

5 ounces bean sprouts

1 red pepper, trimmed, seeded, and cut into thin sticks

6 x ¼-inch pieces mini *chikuwa* (see page 14)

4 cooked and peeled shrimp

2 tablespoons vegetable oil

2 tablespoons dried shallots

1 tablespoon spicy fish powder (see page 15)

1 teaspoon pickled ginger (*gari*, see page 14)

Combine the chicken and the *yakitori* sauce in a bowl. Work gently with your fingers for a few minutes, turning the meat in the sauce. Set aside for at least 30 minutes (1 hour is even better). Remove, reserving the sauce, and cut the chicken into thin slices.

Cook the noodles in a large pot of boiling water for 2–3 minutes or until just tender. Drain and refresh under cold running water. Crack the egg into a large bowl and beat in the *yaki soba* sauce and curry oil. Toss in all the vegetables, *chikuwa*, shrimp, and noodles, and mix until thoroughly combined.

Heat a wok over medium heat for 1–2 minutes or until completely hot and almost smoking and add the oil. Add the chicken and any remaining sauce and stir-fry for 3–4 minutes or until cooked. Add the egg and vegetable mixture and stir-fry for 4–5 minutes until everything is just tender. Divide between 2 plates and top with the shallots, fish powder, and pickled ginger.

Marinating chicken gives the meat much more flavor and the dish overall, a much "bigger" taste. By far the best way to do this is to make up the marinade and place it in a plastic bag with the meat. Massage gently with your hands and set aside in a cool place, overnight if possible.

wagamama ramen

seasonal greens with shrimp, crabstick, tofu, and chicken

If we have a signature dish, this is probably the one. Universally popular, it epitomizes what wagamama is all about. Simple ingredients simply prepared yet delivering oodles of flavor in a nutritious way. This is one of the all-time favorites, a take on the classic noodle dishes eaten at stalls throughout Japan and the inspiration for the first wagamama restaurant.

5 ounces firm tofu
vegetable oil, for frying
9 ounces *ramen* noodles
4 slices *kamaboko-aka* (see page 14)
4 crabsticks
1 egg, hard-boiled
4 cooked and peeled shrimp
2 bok choy, roughly chopped
4 cups chicken stock (see page 17)
2 boneless, skinless chicken breasts
salt and white pepper
12 pieces *menma* (canned bamboo shoots), drained
1 tablespoon *wakame* (see page 15), soaked in warm water for 5 minutes, drained, and roughy chopped
2 scallions, trimmed and finely sliced

Cut the tofu into ½-inch slices and pan-fry in a little oil for about 1 minute on each side until just colored.

Cook the noodles in a large pot of boiling water for 2–3 minutes or until just tender. Drain, refresh under cold running water and drain again. Divide between 2 bowls along with the *kamaboko-aka*, crabsticks, tofu, half an egg each, 2 shrimp each, and the bok choy.

Bring the chicken stock to a boil. Preheat the broiler or a grill pan. Lightly coat the chicken breasts in vegetable oil, season with salt and white pepper, and broil or charbroil for 4 minutes each side or until cooked. Let rest for 5 minutes and slice on the diagonal into ½-inch strips.

To serve, pour the chicken stock over the noodles, lay the chicken strips on top, and garnish with the *menma, wakame,* and scallion slices.

miso ramen

miso soup with chicken, leek, bamboo shoots, and ramen noodles

Miso is a magical food. Made from soybeans and grain, it is similar to yogurt in having living enzymes and has an almost mystical status in Japanese cuisine. There are several different types but personal preference should be the deciding factor. Experiment until you find one you like.

9 ounces *ramen* noodles
4 cups chicken stock (see page 17)
4 ounces *miso* paste (see page 19)
5 ounces boneless, skinless chicken, cut on the diagonal
   into strips ½-inch wide
1 egg, beaten
1 tablespoon cornstarch
salt and white pepper
2 tablespoons vegetable oil
2 garlic cloves, peeled and crushed
1 small carrot, peeled and shredded
½ leek, finely sliced
large handful of bean sprouts
2 teaspoons sugar
2 tablespoons light soy sauce
12 pieces *menma* (canned bamboo shoots), drained
handful of *wakame* (see page 15), soaked in warm water
   for 5 minutes, drained, and roughly chopped
1 teaspoon chilli oil
1 teaspoon sesame seeds, toasted (see page 164)

Cook the noodles in a large pot of boiling water for 2–3 minutes or until just tender. Drain and refresh under cold running water. Place the stock in a pan and bring to a boil. Whisk in the *miso* paste until free of lumps. Cover and remove from the heat.

Combine the chicken, egg, cornstarch, and a seasoning of salt and pepper.

Heat a wok over medium heat for 1–2 minutes or until completely hot and almost smoking, and add the vegetable oil. Add the garlic, stir-fry for 5 seconds, then add the chicken, carrot, leek, and bean sprouts and stir-fry for 3–4 minutes or until slightly caramelized. Add 1 teaspoon salt, the sugar, and soy sauce, and cook for 1 minute.

Divide the noodles between 2 bowls and ladle the stock over them. Top with the vegetables, *menma, wakame*, chili oil, and sesame seeds.

Preparation is the key to cooking the food in this book. Lots of chopping and organizing before the cooking actually takes place. This can mean ingredients lists look long, but you'll already have a lot and what you do need to buy is generally easy to carry home. A good cutting board and sharp knife are essential, but these few utensils mean there is very little to wash afterwards.

chicken rice noodles

with chile and coconut ginger sauce

4 ounces rice noodles

1½ cups coconut ginger sauce
  (see page 25)

3 tablespoons vegetable oil

7 ounces boneless, skinless chicken breast, cut on the
  diagonal into strips ½-inch wide

2 red chiles, trimmed, and finely sliced

1 small onion, peeled and roughly chopped

handful of bean sprouts

½ red pepper, trimmed, seeded, and finely sliced

½ teaspoon salt

½ teaspoon sugar

2 tablespoons light soy sauce

few sprigs of cilantro, for garnishing

1 lime, cut in half, for serving

Cook the noodles in a large pot of boiling water for 2–3 minutes until just tender. Drain and return to the saucepan. Stir in the coconut ginger sauce. Toss well to coat the noodles in the sauce. Cover with a clean dishtowel and set aside.

Heat a wok over medium heat for 1–2 minutes or until completely hot and almost smoking and add the vegetable oil. Add the chicken and stir-fry for 2–3 minutes or until just cooked through. Add the chiles, onion, bean sprouts, and red pepper and continue to stir-fry for another 3 minutes or until the vegetables are beginning to soften. Season with salt, sugar, and soy sauce and continue to stir-fry for another minute.

Divide the noodles between 2 bowls and top with the stir-fry and the cilantro. Serve with a wedge of lime.

Using a wok is relatively easy, but practice is a good idea. Make sure it is well heated—best done over a medium flame for 1 or 2 minutes—then turn the heat up and add the oil, quickly followed by the first group of ingredients.

stir-fries are an incredibly quick way to cook and the short time means all the ingredients retain most of their texture, flavor, and nutrients. The idea is to constantly toss the contents so they stir-fry rather than fry, which is why a large flame is needed to keep the heat as the ingredients move around the wok. You can substitute other poultry for the chicken or vary the vegetables depending upon what you have on hand. We are specific in the restaurants about what goes into a dish, but at home there is lots of leeway to experiment and extend the basic recipe.

marinated chicken stir-fry

with peanuts, lemongrass, soy sauce, and cilantro

2 boneless, skinless chicken breasts, cut on the diagonal into
   strips 1/2-inch wide

2 lemongrass stalks, tough outer leaves removed, very thinly sliced

2–3 red chiles, trimmed and sliced

2 garlic cloves, peeled and crushed

3 tablespoons vegetable oil

2 tablespoons fish sauce (see page 14)

1 small red onion, peeled and cut into 1/2-inch strips

12 snow peas

2 handfuls of bean sprouts

1/2 green pepper, trimmed, seeded, and cubed

1 teaspoon salt

1 teaspoon sugar

1/4 cup salted peanuts, chopped

3 tablespoons light soy sauce

1 1/4 cups water

2 tablespoons cornstarch

2 1/3 cups steamed rice

few sprigs of cilantro, chopped, for garnishing

Put the chicken strips, lemongrass, chile, garlic, 1 tablespoon of the vegetable oil, and the fish sauce in a large bowl. Mix thoroughly, cover, and refrigerate overnight.

Heat a wok over medium heat for 1–2 minutes or until completely hot and almost smoking and add the remaining oil and the red onion. Stir-fry for 1 minute until lightly caramelized. Add the chicken and its marinade and continue stir-frying for 1 minute to seal the meat. Add the snow peas, bean sprouts, and green pepper. Continue stir-frying for another 2 minutes or until the vegetables start to wilt. Add the salt, sugar, and half the peanuts, and stir-fry for another minute.

Add the soy sauce and water. Mix the cornstarch with 2 tablespoons water to make a paste. Remove 2 tablespoons of the sauce from the wok, combine with the cornstarch paste, return to the wok, and toss well. Continue cooking for another 4–5 minutes until the sauce is thick and glossy.

Press the cooked rice into a cup and invert onto 2 plates. Spoon the stir-fry over it and scatter with the remaining peanuts and chopped cilantro.

zasai chicken gohan

stir-fried chicken with Szechuan vegetables, oyster sauce, and sesame oil

1 1/2 tablespoons vegetable oil

7 ounces boneless, skinless chicken breast, cut into strips

1 garlic clove, peeled and crushed

1 ounce pickled cabbage, soaked in cold water for
   15 minutes, then drained

1 ounce Szechuan vegetables (see page 15), soaked in cold water for
   15 minutes, then drained

4 shiitake mushrooms, sliced

4 scallions, trimmed and cut into 1-inch lengths

2/3 cup water

2 teaspoons sugar

1 tablespoon oyster sauce

1 teaspoon salt

2 teaspoons light soy sauce

1/2 teaspoon cornstarch

pinch of white pepper

1 egg, beaten

2 teaspoons sesame oil

2 2/3 cups cooked Japanese short-grain rice

2 teaspoons *zasai* chili sauce (see page 36)

Heat a wok over medium heat for 1–2 minutes or until completely hot and almost smoking and add the vegetable oil. Add the chicken and stir-fry for 3 minutes or until it loses its color. Add the garlic and stir-fry for 5 seconds, then add the pickled vegetables, mushrooms, and scallions. Stir-fry for another 5 seconds and add the water, sugar, oyster sauce, salt, and soy sauce.

Bring to a boil and remove any froth with paper towels. Mix together the cornstarch with 1 tablespoon cold water, the white pepper, and egg, and, when smooth, add to the sauce to thicken. Bring almost to a boil and stir the sesame oil through it.

Divide the rice between 2 plates and add the stir-fried chicken. Top with the *zasai* chili sauce.

5
fish

Tsukiji market, the central fish market in Tokyo, is the largest fish market in the world. I've never seen so much tuna: rows and rows of both fresh and frozen with numbers slapped on to the sides. Quality is everything to the Japanese and some of these tuna are fetching serious prices; arm-waving, constant shouting, and lots of facial expressions do the communicating. I'm simply mesmerized by the fish.

The market is huge and when I tear myself away from the tuna there is everything else you can think of to view: sea bass and sea bream (porgy), salmon and squid, and every size of shrimp imaginable.

Fish is a key source of protein in the Japanese diet; for a small country surrounded by the sea, it was an obvious choice over land-demanding animals like cattle and sheep. At wagamama, we serve a total of over 2,200 pounds of shrimp, salmon, and crabsticks every week, a figure which keeps increasing.

Top of the list for our customers is the seafood *ramen*, a rich and satisfying broth with noodles and shrimp, crabsticks, and squid. It comes with *menma* (pickled bamboo shoots) and *kamaboko-aka*, a small fishcake. The addition of a pickle with fish is very traditional in Japanese cuisine. Alternatives include *gari* (pickled ginger) and *daikon* (white radish).

Many of the wagamama specials are fish based and the following chapter reflects this emphasis. Cod baked in foil, teriyaki sea bass, monkfish *yakitori*—all of these have at one time or another featured on the wagamama menu. But we have also included a few extras: the mackerel with soy and ginger (see page 115), for example, is a great way to serve this much underrated and very healthy fish, and the salmon hot pot (see page 108) is another homey, comforting dish not suited to the busy service needs of the restaurants but one which sits very firmly in the more robust style of Japanese home cooking.

notes on buying fish Freshness is everything when buying fish. Don't be afraid to prod and poke, to question and examine. Ask leading questions: "Is this fresh?" will invariably get a yes, whereas "How fresh is this?" requires a little more thought on the part of your fishseller. An increasing amount of fish we buy is now farmed; unless it states otherwise, this is largely true of most of the salmon, sea bass, and sea bream (porgy) on sale. Farmed fish can be excellent, but its quality can vary hugely and some of it is decidedly below par.

ebi yakitori

stir-fried vegetable skewers with grilled shrimp and dipping sauce

18 raw peeled shrimp

1 zucchini, cut into 1-inch slices

1 orange pepper, trimmed, seeded, and cut into 1-inch chunks

6 thick scallions, trimmed and cut into 1-inch chunks

6 button mushrooms

6 cherry tomatoes

¼ cup *ebi kuzu kiri* sauce (see page 28)

4 ounces *soba* noodles

4 scallions, trimmed and finely sliced

large handful of bean sprouts

2 garlic cloves, peeled and crushed with a little salt

1 teaspoon salt

1 heaped teaspoon sugar

2 tablespoons vegetable oil

6 wooden skewers, soaked in cold water for 2 hours

Thread 3 shrimp on each skewer, alternating with 1 piece of zucchini, 2 pieces of pepper, 2 pieces of thick scallion, 1 mushroom, and 1 tomato. Brush with some of the *ebi kuzu kiri* sauce. Preheat the broiler or a grill pan and cook the *yakitori* for 3–4 minutes, turning frequently, until the shrimp are cooked through.

Cook the noodles in a large pot of boiling water for 2–3 minutes until just tender. Drain thoroughly, then combine in a large bowl with the finely sliced scallions, bean sprouts, garlic, salt, and sugar. Heat a large, heavy frying pan or wok and add the vegetable oil. Add the noodle mixture and stir-fry for 2 minutes until all the ingredients are combined and warmed through. Transfer to 2 plates and top with the cooked shrimp *yakitori*. Drizzle the remaining sauce over them.

It takes quite a while for a grill pan to reach optimal heat. Too hot, and everything will simply burn; not hot enough, and what you lay on top will stew and fail to pick up those attractive lines. Keep the heat medium to hot, and allow a good few minutes for it to reach temperature.

amai udon

stir-fried noodles with shrimp, tofu, and leek

14 ounces *udon* noodles

2 eggs, beaten

1/3 cup *amai* sauce (see page 22)

1 large leek, trimmed and finely sliced

6 cooked peeled shrimp

large handful of bean sprouts

2 tablespoons vegetable oil

4 ounces firm tofu, cut into 10 cubes

juice of 1 lime

2 tablespoons chopped roasted peanuts, for garnishing

Cook the noodles in a large pot of boiling water for 2–3 minutes until just tender. Drain, refresh under cold running water, and reserve.

Put the egg and the *amai* sauce in a large bowl and stir in the leek, shrimp, bean sprouts, and noodles. Heat a wok over medium heat for 1–2 minutes or until completely hot and almost smoking and add the vegetable oil. Add the tofu and stir-fry for 2 minutes or until starting to color.

Tip the contents of the bowl into the wok and stir-fry for 3–4 minutes until the egg is cooked and the leeks are softened.

Divide between 2 bowls, squeeze some lime juice over them, and scatter with the chopped peanuts on top.

stir-fries are one of the most popular cooking methods in our house. My children enjoy the speed as well as the contents. What I really relish is everything tasting its best. Minimal cooking means the snow peas still have crunch as well as flavor, the carrots are still sweet as well as crunchy, and the shrimp have a succulence and sea-salty tang which delights. The lack of dishwashing afterwards also encourages me, but that is to dwell on the mundane.

ebi chili men

stir-fried shrimp with green pepper, carrots, and soba noodles

1 egg
1 teaspoon sesame oil
pinch of white pepper
1 tablespoon cornstarch
12 raw peeled shrimp
2 tablespoons vegetable oil
1 green pepper, trimmed, seeded, and cut into chunks
2 carrots, peeled and sliced on the diagonal
1¼ cups chili sauce (see page 27)
9 ounces *soba* noodles

Combine the egg, sesame oil, white pepper, and cornstarch in a bowl, whisk to form a smooth mixture, and gently stir in the shrimp.

Heat a wok over medium heat for 1–2 minutes or until completely hot and almost smoking and add the vegetable oil. Add the green pepper and carrot and stir-fry for 2–3 minutes or until just tender. Add the shrimp, stir-fry for 30 seconds, then add the chili sauce and bring to a boil. Simmer for 2 minutes, remove from the heat and set aside while you cook the noodles.

Cook the noodles in a large pot of boiling water for 2–3 minutes until just tender. Drain and divide between 2 plates. Top with the shrimp and sauce.

Shrimp in their shells tend to deliver more flavor and texture than their iced-up shell-off cousins. Preparation is slightly more fiddly, but is not that onerous and you can always get somebody to work on this alongside you. If you sauté the shells in the vegetable oil and then discard the shells before you start cooking, it will enhance the flavor of the finished dish.

broiled sea bream (porgy)

with soy sauce and stir-fried garlic noodles

The tang of soy sauce partnered with the nutty, almost sweet flavor of sesame oil is more than a match for this meatiest of fish.

2 x 5-ounce sea bream (porgy) fillets, scaled
2 tablespoons light soy sauce
1 teaspoon sesame oil
4 ounces *soba* noodles
4 scallions, cut into 1-inch lengths
2 teaspoons garlic paste (homemade or bought)
handful of bean sprouts
1 teaspoon salt
1 teaspoon sugar
2 tablespoons vegetable oil

Put the sea bream in a shallow dish and cover with the soy sauce and sesame oil. Cover, then put in the fridge for 2 hours.

Preheat the broiler to medium-high. Cook the noodles in a large pot of boiling water for 2–3 minutes until just tender. Drain thoroughly and refresh under cold water, then combine with the scallions, garlic, bean sprouts, salt, and sugar in a large bowl.

Put the sea bream on a baking sheet skin-side up, reserving the excess marinade. Broil for 5 minutes until cooked through.

Heat a wok over medium heat for 1–2 minutes or until completely hot and almost smoking and add the vegetable oil. Add the noodles and stir-fry for 2 minutes until all the ingredients are heated through, adding in the reserved marinade. Divide the noodles between 2 plates and top with the sea bream.

grilled teriyaki sea bass

with mixed greens and garlic rice

2 x 5-ounce sea bass (grouper) fillets, scaled
¼ cup teriyaki sauce, homemade (see page 28) or bought
1 cup rice
1 tablespoon vegetable oil
pinch of salt
large handful of mixed salad greens
1 tablespoon shredded carrot or *daikon* (mooli)
¼ cup garlic herb oil (see page 35)

Place the sea bass fillets in a bowl with 2 tablespoons of the teriyaki sauce. Toss gently and set aside. Cook the rice in a pan of boiling water for 8 minutes (or according to the package instructions) until just tender, then drain.

Heat a grill pan until really hot and lightly oil with paper towels dipped in vegetable oil. Season the sea bass with the salt, then cook, skin-side down, for 2 minutes. Turn over and cook for 1 minute until done.

Press the rice into a cup and invert onto 2 plates. Combine the salad greens and carrot or *daikon,* and place a handful alongside the rice. Drizzle the garlic herb oil over it along with 1 tablespoon of the teriyaki sauce for each plate. Top with the sea bass and a little extra teriyaki sauce.

For the love of God, open a wagamama in New York!
Mike, USA

home-cured spiced swordfish steak

grilled swordfish, ramen noodles, and baby vegetables

Vegetables poached in a light stock, the gutsy flavor of just-cooked swordfish, and the soothing comfort of noodles. Simplicity at its best and everything tasting of itself; pure and easy.

2 scant teaspoons coarse sea salt or kosher salt

2 x 6-ounce swordfish steaks

pinch of ground black pepper

1 teaspoon finely chopped garlic

1 red chile, trimmed, seeded, and sliced

2 sprigs of cilantro, finely chopped

1 tablespoon lime juice

4 cups vegetable stock (see page 18)

3 ounces baby vegetables (baby corn cobs, sugarsnap peas, or snow peas)

10½ ounces *ramen* noodles

a little vegetable oil

4 scallions, trimmed and sliced, for garnishing

Line a tray with plastic wrap, place half the salt on the plastic, and put the sword-fish on top. Cover with the remaining salt, the black pepper, garlic, sliced red chile and cilantro. Pour the lime juice over it. Cover with more plastic wrap and place another tray with weights (or something heavy) on it and let it marinate overnight in the fridge.

The following day, heat the stock and cook the baby vegetables for 2–3 minutes or until tender. Cook the noodles in a large pot of boiling water for 2–3 minutes until just tender, then drain thoroughly. Divide between 2 bowls and ladle the stock and vegetables over them.

Brush the salt mixture off the swordfish. Heat a grill pan, lightly oil it using paper towels dipped in vegetable oil, and cook the swordfish for 2–3 minutes on each side or until opaque right through. Slice the steaks, place on top of the noodles, and sprinkle the scallion slices on top.

Oil the grill pan lightly to avoid a kitchen full of smoke. Some fumes are inevitable, but the idea is to be able to see what you are doing and not be arguing with firemen.

fish is surely the ultimate fast food for those of us interested in real food; easy to prepare, quick to cook, and full of texture and flavor. No wonder this is the largest chapter in the book. Fish is an ingredient as friendly to a wok as a saucepan of hot broth, and up for marinating as keenly as being seared in a pan of hot oil.

poached cod with shiitake

and soy sauce

2 tablespoons butter

5-ounce cod fillets

2 scallions, trimmed and finely sliced

¼ green pepper, trimmed, seeded, and cut into thin strips

handful of shiitake mushrooms, finely sliced

1 tablespoon sake

salt and white pepper

2 teaspoons light soy sauce

2 x aluminum foil squares about three times the size of the cod fillets

for serving

mixed salad greens

steamed rice or bean thread vermicelli

Preheat the oven to 400°F. Lay the foil squares on a board, shiny-side down. Using half the butter, grease an area just larger than the size of the cod fillets.

Put the cod on the foil, skin-side down, and top with the scallions, green pepper, and shiitake mushrooms. Dot with the remaining butter and the sake and season with salt and pepper.

Wrap the foil tightly to form a sealed package. Put in a roasting pan and pour in enough hot water to come half way up the sides. Place in the center of the oven for about 10 minutes, or until cooked. Open the foil packets carefully and drizzle in the soy sauce. Serve with a simple salad and steamed rice or glass vermicelli.

Butter, soy sauce and sake are a winning combination. They shouldn't work—butter is hardly an Eastern ingredient —but pry open the sealed tin-foil after cooking and you will be enveloped in a cloud of steam, heady with rich and exotic aromas.

sweet miso cod

grilled marinated cod, black sesame seeds, and seaweed rice

Miso lends this dish an unmistakably meaty quality making it somehow much bigger. Which miso you use in the dressing is a matter of personal preference. Experiment and see which one you prefer—they all contain subtle differences.

2 tablespoons dried *wakame* (see page 15), soaked in warm water
   for 5 minutes
2 x 5-ounce cod fillets
4 fluid ounces sweet *miso* dressing (see page 35)
²/₃ cup rice
a little vegetable oil
½ teaspoon black sesame seeds, for sprinkling

Drain the *wakame*, squeeze gently, and roughly chop. Set aside, for the garnish.

Put the cod in a shallow bowl and pour the sweet *miso* dressing over it. Place in the fridge for 1 hour or overnight if possible. Cook the rice in a large pan of boiling water until tender, then drain and keep warm.

Heat a grill pan until hot and lightly oil it with paper towels dipped in vegetable oil. Put the cod fillets on the grill pan and cook, skin-side down, for 5 minutes. Turn over and cook for another 2 minutes, or until opaque right through. The *miso* should be colored, but not black.

Divide the rice between 2 plates and sprinkle the black sesame seeds over it. Put the seaweed on top and finally the *miso* cod.

Bench seating and communal tables are hallmarks of wagamama. They make for a bustling, exciting atmosphere and lots of exchange. Regulars help newcomers and it allows groups to shrink and grow with ease.

kai sen udon

stir-fried seafood with oyster sauce and udon noodles

You can vary the seafood used here, but the shapes are half the fun; squid, shrimp, and scallops all lending their own texture and flavor wrapped up in a broth heady with the flavors of soy and sesame oil, garlic and oyster sauce.

14 ounces *udon* noodles

2 teaspoons cornstarch

2 tablespoons vegetable oil

2 garlic cloves, peeled and crushed

1 red pepper, trimmed, and very thinly sliced

12 baby squid, cleaned

4 uncooked peeled shrimp

8 bay scallops

12 slices of *chikuwa* (see page 14)

2 tablespoons *shaoshing* wine (see page 15)

⅔ cup water

1 teaspoon salt

1 teaspoon sugar

2 tablepoons oyster sauce

1 tablespoon light soy sauce

2 ounces bok choy, roughly chopped

2 teaspoons sesame oil

1 crabstick, shredded, for garnishing

large pinch of crushed black pepper

Cook the noodles in a large pot of boiling water for 2–3 minutes until just tender. Drain thoroughly, refresh under cold water, and set aside. Mix 2 tablespoons cold water with the cornstarch.

Heat a wok over medium heat for 1–2 minutes or until completely hot and almost smoking and add the vegetable oil. Stir-fry the garlic for 5 seconds, being careful not to let it brown. Add the red pepper and stir-fry for 1 minute, then add the seafood and stir-fry for 30 seconds. Pour in the wine and water and quickly bring to a boil. Add the salt, sugar, oyster sauce, and soy sauce. Add the bok choy, then the corn-starch paste, and bring back to a boil—the sauce should have a coating consistency. Stir the sesame oil through it.

Divide the noodles between 2 plates and top with the contents of the wok. Top with the shredded crabstick and crushed black pepper.

Bok choy is widely used in dishes throughout this book. Like spinach, its leaves melt to a silky texture, but the stems add crunch and body. It keeps well in the fridge for 2–3 days.

smoked haddock ramen

with chives and baby vegetables

8 ounces smoked haddock

1 tablespoon finely chopped Chinese chives (regular chives can be used, though they lack the garlic kick of Chinese chives)

large pinch of black pepper

9 ounces *ramen* noodles

4 cups *miso* soup (see page 46)

2 ounces babycorn

2 ounces zucchini

large handful of watercress

1 ounce *kombu* (see page 14), soaked in warm water for 5 minutes and drained

12 pieces *menma* (canned bamboo shoots), drained

Put the haddock, skin-side down, in a pan. Cover with water, put on the lid, bring to a boil, and simmer for 5 minutes or until opaque right through. Gently flake the fish, removing any bones and skin, and discard the cooking liquor. Add the Chinese chives and black pepper.

Cook the noodles in a large pot of boiling water for 2–3 minutes until just tender. Drain thoroughly, refresh under cold water, and divide between 2 bowls. Heat the *miso* soup until boiling, then add the baby vegetables, and cook for 3 minutes, or until tender. Ladle the soup and vegetables over the noodles and top with the watercress and haddock, *kombu,* and *menma.*

It really does make sense to assemble all the ingredients for a recipe before you start. The cooking process is not helped if you are rushing around trying to find something while your wok catches fire! Take time over the preparation and all will follow in one seamless stream.

smoked fish should be a dusty, elegant color, not strong and vivid. If you encounter the latter, it has probably been dyed. There is little reason for this beyond a perception that some customers prefer it. The color is hardly attractive and what is the point?

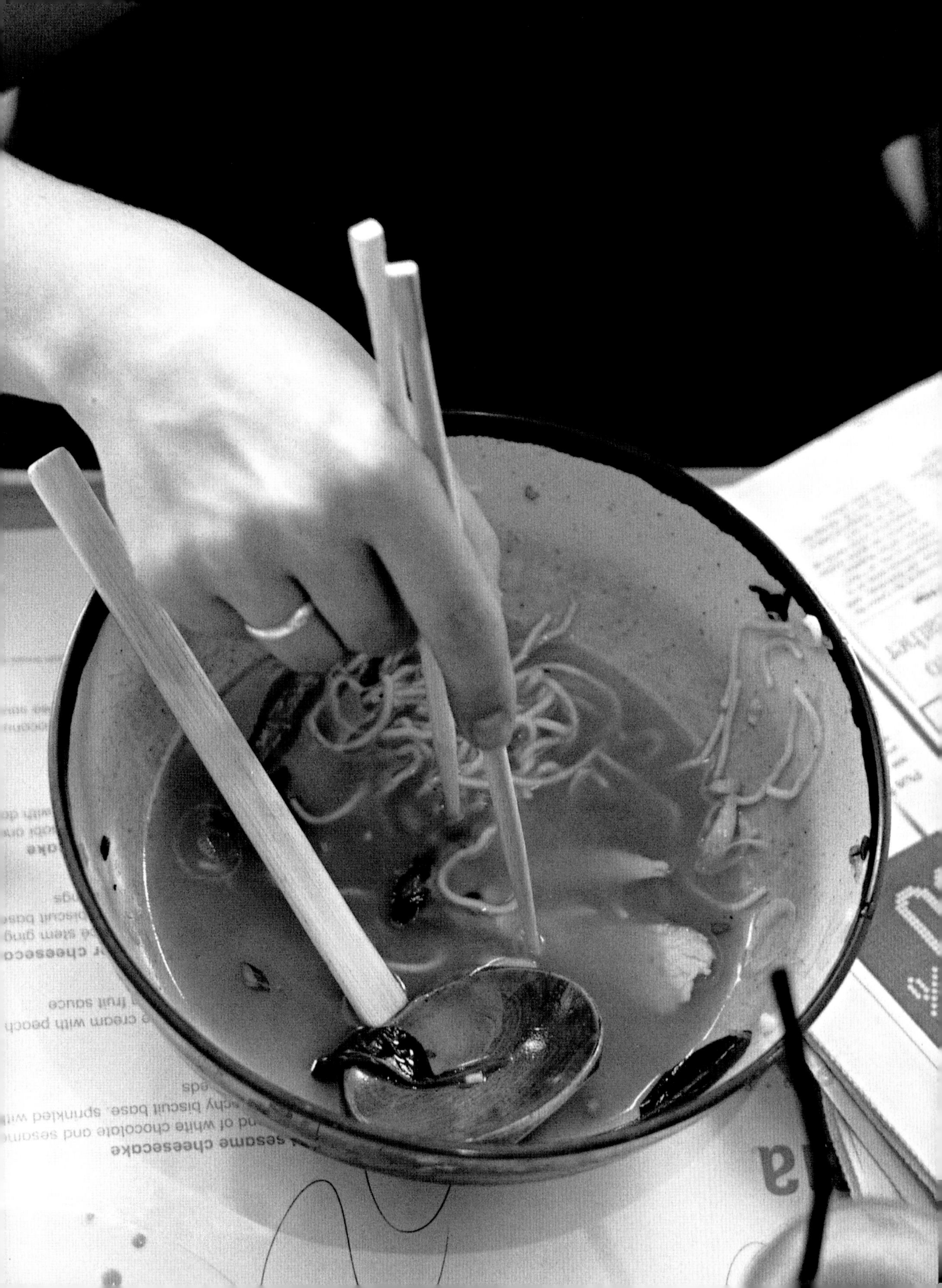

suzuki amiyaki soba

sea bass, bok choy, sesame oil, and cilantro

6 ounces *soba* noodles

2 tablespoons vegetable oil

1 red onion, peeled and thinly sliced

2 baby bok choy, trimmed and stems sliced

large handful of bean sprouts

2 garlic cloves, peeled and finely chopped

2 teaspoons sesame oil

2 tablespoons *yasai soba* salad dressing (see page 39)

2 x 5-ounce sea bass or grouper fillets

salt and white pepper

1 tablespoon finely chopped shallots, for sprinkling

2 sprigs of cilantro, for garnishing

1 lime, cut into wedges, for serving

Previous spread, right: If you can use chopsticks that's all well and good, but we provide cutlery for anyone shy of trying. All the staff will happily show you, however, and those paper placemats are ideal for covering up any early mistakes.

Cook the noodles in a large pot of boiling water for 2–3 minutes until just tender. Drain thoroughly and refresh under cold running water.

Heat a wok or heavy frying pan over medium heat for 1–2 minutes or until completely hot and almost smoking and add 1 tablespoon of the vegetable oil. Add the red onion, bok choy, bean sprouts, and garlic, and stir-fry for 1 minute until just warmed through, moving the vegetables around constantly so that the garlic does not burn. Remove from the heat.

Toss the noodles with the vegetables, sesame oil, and the *yasai soba* salad dressing in a large bowl until thoroughly combined and cover with a clean dishtowel.

Season the sea bass fillets with salt and pepper. Heat a heavy frying pan and add the remaining vegetable oil. Add the fish, skin-side down, and cook for 2–3 minutes until almost opaque. Turn over and cook for another minute.

Divide the noodles and vegetables between 2 bowls and top with the sea bass. Sprinkle with the shallots and cilantro, and serve with lime wedges.

hake tempura

deep-fried hake with ramen noodles, watercress, and chile

There is nothing difficult about making tempura dishes; just make sure you use ice-cold beer and pure vegetable oil and don't over-whisk the batter mixture. That way, it will remain light and airy rather than gooey and elastic.

½ egg, beaten
½ cup cold beer
pinch of baking soda
salt and white pepper
⅓ cup plain flour, plus extra for dusting
1¾ cups vegetable oil
14 ounces hake, skinned and cut into 8 large chunks
10½ ounces *ramen* noodles
4 cups vegetable stock (see page 18)
small handful of watercress
handful of bean sprouts
6 scallions, trimmed and cut on the diagonal into 1-inch slices
1 red chile, trimmed and sliced

Cook the noodles in a large pot of boiling water for 2–3 minutes until just tender. Drain thoroughly, refresh under cold water, and divide between 2 bowls.

Combine the egg, beer, baking soda, a seasoning of salt and pepper, and the flour in a bowl and whisk to form a light batter. Heat the oil in a heavy saucepan until a little batter dropped into it sinks to the bottom and then rises up. (If the batter stays down, the oil is not hot enough.)

Dip the fish in the flour for dusting and then in the batter, and deep-fry 4 pieces at a time for 5 minutes until golden and cooked through. Make sure that none sticks to the bottom of the pan, which can happen if the oil is not quite hot enough.

In another pan, bring the vegetable stock to a boil and ladle it over the noodles. Top with the watercress and beansprouts. Put the fish pieces on top and sprinkle with the slices of scallion and chile.

salmon ramen

teriyaki salmon with baby vegetables, miso soup, and noodles

9 ounces *ramen* noodles

2 ounces baby vegetables (baby corn cobs, sugarsnap peas, or snow peas)
  or bok choy

a little vegetable oil

2 x 5-ounce salmon fillets

2 tablespoons teriyaki sauce, homemade (see page 28) or store-bought

4 cups chicken or vegetable stock (see pages 17 and 18)

4$\frac{1}{2}$ tablespoons *miso* paste (see page 19)

12 pieces *menma* (canned bamboo shoots), drained

4 scallions, trimmed and finely sliced

Cook the noodles in a large pot of boiling water for 2–3 minutes until just tender. Add the baby vegetables or bok choy for the final 2 minutes to cook until just tender. Drain and refresh everything under cold running water.

Heat a heavy frying pan or grill pan until hot, lightly oil with paper towels dipped in vegetable oil, and cook the salmon for 2 minutes on each side, or until opaque right through. Warm the teriyaki sauce in a small pan and brush the salmon with it.

Bring the stock to a boil in a large pan, then whisk in the *miso* paste until smooth. Divide the noodles and vegetables between 2 bowls and ladle the stock over them. Top with the salmon, *menma,* and scallion slices.

Oodles of noodles: they are absolutely central to wagamama. Typically the restaurants serve over 13,000 pounds of ramen noodles in a week.

sake amiyaki gohan

broiled salmon with bok choy, ginger, oyster sauce, and steamed rice

5-ounce salmon fillets

2 teaspoons vegetable oil

1 garlic clove, peeled, finely chopped, and crushed with a little salt

1 tablespoon peeled and grated fresh ginger root

1 small red onion, peeled and cut into chunks

1 red chile, trimmed and thinly sliced

2 heads of bok choy, halved lengthwise

2¼ cups boiling water

1 tablespoon oyster sauce

2 teaspoons light soy sauce

1 teaspoon salt

1 tablespoon sugar

14 snow peas

1 tablespoon *shaoshing* wine (see page 15)

1 tablespoon sesame oil

1 teaspoon cornstarch

steamed Japanese rice, for serving

Preheat the broiler. Put the salmon on a lightly oiled baking tray, skin-side down, and broil for 2 minutes, then turn over and cook for another 6 minutes.

Heat a wok or large frying pan over medium heat for 1–2 minutes or until completely hot and almost smoking and add the vegetable oil. Stir fry the garlic and ginger for 5 seconds, taking care not to let them color too much. Add the onion, chile, and bok choy and stir-fry for another 30 seconds. Pour in the water, oyster, and soy sauces, and add the salt and sugar. Bring to a boil. Add the snow peas and cook for 1 minute. Splash in the wine and sesame oil.

Mix the cornstarch to a paste with a little cold water. Remove 2 tablespoons of the sauce from the wok and combine with the paste. Return to the wok and stir over a medium heat for 5 minutes or until you have a shiny sauce.

Place a portion of steamed rice on 2 plates and top with the salmon. Pour the sauce from the wok over it.

The skin on fish is too often discarded. Seasoned and cooked correctly so it crisps up, it provides both a textural and flavor contrast, as well as dramatic color variation.

salmon korroke

salmon cakes with amai sauce, mixed greens, and wakame

makes 6 cakes

7 ounces floury potatoes, peeled
and quartered

10½ ounces salmon fillet

3 tablespoons canned corn, drained

7 tablepoons vegetable oil

1 onion, peeled and finely chopped

1 small carrot, peeled and finely chopped

¼ cup frozen peas

salt and white pepper

3 eggs

4 heaped tablespoons flour

2 ounces *panko* bread crumbs (see page 15)

2 tablespoons *amai* sauce (see page 22)

2 tablespoons wagamama salad dressing (see page 32)

2 large handfuls of mixed salad greens

2 tablespoons *wakame*, soaked in warm water for 5 minutes, for garnishing

The secret to a really good fishcake is to ensure the fish remains the key focus. That, and a light hand in the forming. The idea is to keep the texture elegant and fluffy and allow the flavor of the fish to come through. Success is all in the detail.

Put the potatoes in cold water, cover, bring to a boil, and cook for 10 minutes. Add the salmon and cook for 7 minutes until it is cooked right through and the potatoes are tender. Lift out the salmon and flake it. Drain the potatoes, return to the pan, and mash them.

While the potatoes and salmon are cooking, heat a wok over medium heat for 1–2 minutes until hot and almost smoking and add 2 tablespoons of the oil. Add the onion, cover, and cook over a very low heat for 5 minutes until translucent, stirring to make sure it doesn't stick and color. Add the carrot and cook for another 5 minutes; add the peas for the last minute.

Combine the salmon and potatoes in a bowl along with the onion mixture and the corn. Season thoroughly and add 2 of the eggs. Beat into the mixture and combine thoroughly. Divide into 6 equal portions and shape into fishcakes.

Put the flour in one bowl, the remaining egg, beaten, in another, and the breadcrumbs in a third. Dip the salmon cakes first in the flour, then in the egg, and finally in the crumbs.

Heat a large frying pan, then add the remaining oil. Fry the fishcakes over medium-low heat for 2–3 minutes on each side until golden. Drain on paper towels. Heat the *amai* sauce. Divide the salmon cakes between 2 plates and drizzle the sauce around the plates.

Mix the dressing with the salad greens and place small mounds on top of the salmon cakes. Garnish with *wakame*.

salmon hot pot

with carrot, leek, soy sauce, and brown rice

This is one of the few dishes in the book that doesn't feature on the wagamama menu, but works beautifully in the home setting where 30 minutes cooking time isn't a problem.

14 ounces salmon

2 tablespoons vegetable oil

1 leek, trimmed and finely sliced

1 tablespoon finely chopped shallot

1 carrot, peeled and finely chopped

1 stalk celery, peeled of any strings and finely chopped

1 teaspoon sugar

2 garlic cloves, peeled and finely chopped

salt and white pepper

$1/3$ cup light soy sauce

$2^{1}/3$ cups cooked brown rice

Preheat the oven to 350°F. Remove any skin and bones from the salmon and cut the flesh into bite-sized pieces. Heat the oil in a heavy, ovenproof pan, and when it is hot add the leek, shallot, carrot, and celery, and sauté gently for 10 minutes. Add the sugar and garlic, cook for another minute and then add the fish and season with salt and pepper. Pour the soy sauce over it, add $1/4$ cup of water, cover, and bake in the oven for 15 minutes. Remove and let rest for 5 minutes. Divide the rice between 2 bowls and ladle the salmon hot pot over it.

Chefs go through a lot of training when they start. Many are new to kitchens, or have worked in places where systems are not important. For wagamama, quality is our first priority and we must deliver that consistently well. Every dish has a procedure to follow, so that each time it comes out looking and tasting consistently good.

spiced sake soba

salmon soba with oyster mushrooms and red and yellow peppers

8 ounces *soba* noodles

2 tablespoons vegetable oil

2 x 5-ounce salmon fillets

salt

½ yellow pepper, trimmed, seeded, and sliced

½ red pepper, trimmed, seeded, and sliced

½ red onion, peeled and sliced

handful of oyster mushrooms

large handful of bean sprouts

1 zucchini, cut into thin strips

1 tablespoon rice vinegar

2 tablespoons chili oil

1 tablespoon fried onions

2 tablespoons *yaki soba* sauce (see page 32)

2 eggs, beaten

1 teaspoon sesame seeds, for sprinkling

1 lemon, cut into wedges, for serving

Cook the noodles in a large pot of boiling water for 2–3 minutes until just tender. Drain and refresh under cold running water. Heat a frying pan until hot and add 1 tablespoon of the vegetable oil. Season the skin on the salmon with salt, then cook, skin-side down, over a high heat for 5 minutes, then turn over and cook for 2 minutes on the other side. Set aside.

Meanwhile, heat a wok or large frying pan over medium heat for 1–2 minutes or until completely hot and almost smoking and add the remaining vegetable oil. Add the peppers, onion, mushrooms, bean sprouts, zucchini, rice vinegar, chili oil and the fried onions. Stir-fry for 5–8 minutes until tender. Stir in the noodles and *yaki soba* sauce and cook for 1–2 minutes.

Add the eggs and stir-fry for another minute or until the eggs are cooked. Divide between 2 dishes, scatter the sesame seeds over them and top with the salmon fillet and a lemon wedge.

our website is a central part of our communications strategy. Talk to us and we will talk to you. We fundamentally believe in listening and responding to you. For us the customer really does come first.

yaki soba

stir-fried chicken and shrimp with soba noodles and pickled ginger

This dish has become known as *yaki soba* even though, traditionally, it doesn't use *soba* noodles. You can use *ramen* instead if you prefer, as we do in the restaurants.

4 ounces *soba* noodles
2 tablespoons *yaki soba* sauce (see page 32)
1 small onion, peeled and cut into half-moon slices
4 scallions, trimmed and cut into 1-inch lengths
large handful of bean sprouts
15 small cooked peeled shrimp
2 tablespoons vegetable oil
1 boneless, skinless chicken breast, cut into strips
½ red pepper, trimmed, seeded, and cubed
½ green pepper, trimmed, seeded, and cubed
2 eggs, beaten

for serving

2 tablespoons pickled ginger (*gari*, see page 14)
1 tablespoon dried shallots
½ teaspoon toasted sesame seeds (see page 164)

Cook the noodles in a large pot of boiling water for 2–3 minutes until just tender. Drain and refresh under cold running water.

Put the *yaki soba* sauce, the onion, scallions, bean sprouts, and shrimp in a large bowl and mix in the noodles.

Heat a wok over medium heat for 1–2 minutes or until completely hot and almost smoking and add the vegetable oil. Add the chicken and red and green peppers, and stir-fry for 2 minutes. Add the noodles and vegetables to the wok and stir-fry quickly for 3 minutes until warmed through. Add the eggs and continue to stir-fry for another minute or until the eggs are just cooked. Serve with the pickled ginger, shallots, and sesame seeds.

A wok with one long handle is easier to toss and that is what's so crucial to stir frying because it keeps the ingredients moving constantly round the pan. The flicking of the wrist is almost impossible with two handles but then some people prefer to stir and there is nothing wrong with that.

in Japan there are four main types of noodles: *ramen* (Chinese style), *soba* (whole-wheatl), *udon* (thick and white), and *somen* (thin and white). Does it matter which one you use? Not really, but as with pasta, spaghetti Bolognese and meatballs just isn't the same if you don't use spaghetti.

monkfish yakitori

with green-tea soba noodles, soy sauce, ginger, and lime

Monkfish, also known as angler fish, is perfect at picking up strong flavors and is a dream to broil. If you want a variation on this recipe, try using scallops, which are even more succulent. If you cannot find lemongrass stalks, wooden skewers make perfectly good substitutes.

4 scallions, trimmed and cut into 1½-inch lengths

10½ ounces monkfish (angler fish), cleaned, boned, and cut into 1-inch slices

2 lemongrass stalks, outer leaves removed, split lengthwise

1 tablespoon vegetable oil

salt and white pepper

9 ounces *soba* noodles

3 cups tea green tea

generous handful of roughly chopped choy sum (see page 14)

generous handful of bean sprouts

1 garlic clove, peeled and crushed

1 green chile, trimmed and sliced

1 teaspoon chopped cilantro

1 red onion, peeled and finely sliced

for the dressing

1 tablespoon olive oil

2 tablespoons light soy sauce

½ teaspoon peeled and grated fresh ginger root

juice of 1 lime

½ teaspoon sugar

These yakitori make fantastic party food when served on their own. Just the thing to partner ice-cold beers.

Preheat the broiler. Make a small slit in each cut length of scallion. Thread the monkfish and scallion pieces equally onto the 2 lemongrass stalks. Place on a baking tray and brush with the vegetable oil. Season with salt and pepper.

Place the tray of monkfish *yakitori* under the hot broiler and cook for 6–7 minutes, turning the stalks once.

Meanwhile, cook the noodles in a large pot of boiling hot green tea for 2–3 minutes until just tender. Drain thoroughly and refresh under cold running water. Combine the remaining ingredients, toss with the noodles in a large bowl, and divide between 2 plates.

Top the noodle mixture with the monkfish. Mix together all the dressing ingredients and drizzle them over it.

seafood ramen

with menma, snow peas, noodles, and scallions

Seafood *ramen* is another top seller, the perfect fast food offering a nutritionally complete meal in a bowl. One-stop dining of the best kind, and able to provide you with energy that you will start to burn immediately.

9 ounces *ramen* noodles
4 cups chicken or vegetable stock (see pages 17 and 18)
a small handful snowpeas and baby corn
10 small squid, prepared
4 cooked tiger shrimp, peeled and deveined
2 crabsticks
2 x ¼-inch slices *kamaboko-aka* (see page 14)
12 pieces *menma* (canned bamboo shoots), drained
1 ounce *wakame* (see page 15), soaked in warm water for
   5 minutes and roughly chopped
4 scallions, trimmed and finely sliced

Cook the noodles in a large pot of boiling water for 2–3 minutes until tender. Drain thoroughly and refresh under cold running water.

Bring the stock to a boil in a large pan. Add the snow peas and baby corn and cook for 3 minutes until just tender. Add the squid, cook for 1 minute, then add the shrimp and remove the pan from the heat.

Divide the noodles between 2 bowls and ladle the stock, vegetables, and fish over them. Top with the crabsticks, *kamaboko-aka*, *menma*, *wakame*, and scallions.

Food this good, this fast? Until I tasted a bowl of your chicken ramen, I thought all fast food was rubbish. Thanks for breaking the mold.
Françoise, Paris

mackerel with soy and ginger

with sake, mirin, and Japanese rice

1 mackerel, scaled, cleaned, and filleted

for the marinade

3 tablespoons light soy sauce

1-inch piece of fresh ginger root, peeled and grated

1 garlic clove, peeled, chopped, and mashed to a paste with a little salt

2 tablespoons sake

1 tablespoon *mirin* (see page 14)

1 teaspoon sugar

for serving

2⅓ cups cooked Japanese short-grain rice

pickles (see page 15)

Place the fish fillets, skin-side down, in a flat china dish or non-metallic container. Mix together all the marinade ingredients and spoon them over the fish. Set aside for 1 hour.

Preheat the broiler, then cook the marinated fillets, skin-side down, for 2 minutes. Turn over, brush with extra marinade, and broil for another 3–4 minutes or until the skin is well blistered and golden.

Divide the rice between 2 plates, top with a fillet of mackerel each, and serve with a portion of pickles.

We don't stand on ceremony in the restaurants. You cannot book a table, no smoking is allowed, and your order is keyed into a hand-held computer. That way you get to sit down quickly and your food can arrive in moments. It is designed to be easy and accessible.

6
meat

At the heart of wagamama lies a culinary holy trinity: a bowl of noodles, the soup or broth base, and a topping. When founder Alan Yau was working on the original scheme for the first restaurant in Streatham Street in London's Bloomsbury, it was essentially this dish—eaten at noodle stalls throughout the Far East but particularly in Tokyo—he saw as the core of the menu. It has remained there ever since.

In Tokyo these stalls are very simple affairs: a bench and a few pots holding the hot stock, the noodles, and the various toppings. Good food prepared fast—exactly what many of us want at home. Unlike many so-called fast-food restaurants, the huge benefit of this way of cooking is that the quality is high and it remains healthy. At wagamama, we spend a great deal of time and attention finding prime ingredients and doing as little to them as possible. We might marinate meat to enhance its flavor, but apart from that, the inherent qualities of the dish come from the other ingredients added—a little chile, perhaps, lemongrass, red peppers, or finely sliced scallion.

When you try these recipes at home, the time for marinating the meat may be short, but don't let that put you off. Half an hour will make a substantial difference. The dish won't taste quite the same, or have the same depth of flavor, but it will still be delicious.

You might be surprised to see just how little meat is used in the following recipes. This is very much in keeping with the whole noodle philosophy and not that far from the Italian view on meat in pasta dishes: a little goes a long way. With our increasing awareness of the need for healthier eating, the idea of less, but better quality, is central to our thinking.

Quality and consistency are what wagamama is all about. As we have expanded, consistency has come to play a major role—it has to. Driving that knowledge back into the company is aimed at one key target: maintaining and improving quality. This same attention to detail is carried through in these recipes. Restaurant recipes (we call them specs) seldom automatically transfer to a domestic setting, so we have developed and tested each one in a domestic kitchen to ensure they work properly.

Kaizen is the Japanese word for gradual, ongoing, and simple improvements. In essence, it means you do things, learn things, then you do more things. Never standing still may be a more straightforward explanation but that suggests a random approach. Cooking is so much about confidence, and that can only be attained by doing, learning, and then moving on.

Although the list of ingredients in some of these recipes may seem long, many of them will be—or can be—already in stock. A bowl of noodles today, *teppanyaki* tomorrow.

shichimi spiced duck ramen

noodle soup with spring greens

2 x 5-ounce boneless duck breasts (skin on)

2 teaspoons *shichimi* (see page 15)

½ teaspoon salt

½ teaspoon sugar

9 ounces *ramen* noodles

4 cups vegetable stock (see page 18)

2 handfuls of roughly chopped bok choy or baby spinach

4 scallions, trimmed and finely sliced, for garnishing

Prepare the duck by lightly scoring the skin. Mix the *shichimi*, salt, and sugar together in a shallow dish and lay the duck breasts in the marinade, skin-side down. Put a plate on top and weigh it down with something heavy—say a couple of unopened cans of baked beans. Place the weighted duck in the fridge and marinate for 1 hour or if possible, overnight.

To cook the duck, preheat a grill pan or frying pan over medium heat for 1–2 minutes until hot and almost smoking. Cook the duck, skin-side down, for 5 minutes, then turn it over and cook on the other side for 3 minutes or until cooked. Set aside to rest for 5 minutes.

To serve, cook the noodles in a large pot of boiling water for 2–3 minutes or until just tender. Drain and divide between 2 bowls. In a large saucepan, bring the vegetable stock to a boil, add the bok choy and cook for 1 minute, then ladle it over the noodles. Check the seasoning. Thinly slice the duck at a slight angle and place on top, along with the scallions.

Far left: The recipes in this book contain a lot of chopping and a sharp knife is essential. You can spend a great deal of money on one (pricey kitchen stores), or not very much at all (ethnic supermarkets and simply replace often), depending upon your budget. Left: Noodles ready to go. Cooking them ahead of finally composing the dish really does make life a lot easier.

chili beef ramen

with bean sprouts, red onion, and lime

5 ounces bean sprouts

9 ounces *ramen* noodles

12 ounces sirloin steak, ¾-inch thick, in the piece

a little vegetable oil

a little teriyaki sauce, for brushing

4 cups chicken or vegetable stock (see page 17)

2 tablespoons chili *ramen* sauce (see page 23)

4 scallions, trimmed and sliced

1 red chile, trimmed, seeded, and sliced lengthwise

½ red onion, peeled and very thinly sliced

1 lime, quartered

6 sprigs of cilantro

Blanch the bean sprouts in a large pot of boiling water for 10 seconds. Drain, reserving the water, and refresh in cold running water. Cook the noodles in the reserved boiling water for 2–3 minutes or until just tender. Drain thoroughly and refresh under cold running water.

Heat a grill pan or frying pan over medium heat for 1–2 minutes until hot and almost smoking. Lightly rub the steak with oil, then cook for 2 minutes on each side until medium rare. Remove from the pan, brush with the teriyaki sauce, and keep it warm while it rests for 3–4 minutes. Slice on the diagonal.

Divide the noodles between 2 bowls. In a saucepan, heat the stock, stir in the chili *ramen* sauce, then ladle it over the noodles. Top with the beef, bean sprouts, scallions, chile, red onion, 2 lime quarters, and the cilantro.

It's in the bowl. Ramen continues to be one of our top sellers, a complete meal in one; fast and nutritious; simple food at its best.

chiles are one of those ingredients about which people tend to feel strongly. Love them or hate them, what is wonderful is how easy it is to include them or leave them out. In the restaurants, we tend to use them sparingly—people can always ask for more or add chili sauce if they want that extra kick. But at home, you can do what you want.

pork and beef cabbage rolls

with scallion, chile, and soy sauce

8 large Chinese (napa) cabbage outer leaves
salt and black pepper
¼ cup lean ground pork
¼ cup lean ground beef
1 small onion, peeled and chopped
4 scallions, trimmed and chopped
1 green chile, trimmed, seeded, and finely chopped
⅓ cup cooked Japanese rice
4 toothpicks

for the stock
1 tablespoon *mirin* (see page 14)
2½ cups *dashi*, made with *dashi no moto* (see page 14)
1 tablespoon light soy sauce
1 tablespoon sake

Cook the cabbage leaves in a large pot of lightly salted boiling water for 3 minutes. Drain and lay flat on a clean dishtowel to cool. Cut a triangle out of the thickest end of the stems (you can leave some stem) and discard. In a large bowl, combine the ground pork and beef, onion, scallions, and chile. Lightly season with salt and black pepper, then add the cooked rice and mix to bind everything together.

Overlap 2 cabbage leaves on a cutting board, place a quarter of the meat filling in the center, and fold up the leaves to form a wrap. Secure with a toothpick. Prepare three other wraps in the same way.

Bring the *mirin*, *dashi*, soy sauce, sake, and a pinch of salt to a boil, then lower the heat to a simmer. Add the cabbage rolls and cover with a lid. Simmer for 40 minutes or until the meat is cooked. To serve, lift out of the stock, remove the toothpicks, and slice in half. Place in 2 serving bowls and ladle some of the stock over them.

These wraps also make fantastic canapés. You can make the stuffed rolls in advance but stop before you cook them because the cabbage tends to discolor an hour or so after it is cooked.

pork belly hot pot

with mixed vegetables, sake, and miso

2 ounces *konnyaku*, (see page 14), optional

3 tablespoons vegetable oil

5 ounces belly pork, cut into thin strips (alternatively use bacon)

1 red onion, peeled and sliced

4 ounces *daikon* (mooli), peeled and shredded

2 carrots, peeled and grated

4 ounces sweet potato, peeled and julienned

4 shiitake mushrooms

8 baby corn cobs, cut in half lengthwise

1¾ cups *dashi*, made with *dashi no moto* (see page 14)

1 tablespoon sake

1½ tablespoons *miso* paste (see page 19)

If using *konnyaku*, place in a small pan and cover with water. Bring to a boil over medium heat, then drain and let cool. Roughly chop the *konnyaku*.

Heat a wok over medium heat for 1–2 minutes or until completely hot and almost smoking and add the vegetable oil. Add the pork and stir-fry for 1 minute. Add the vegetables and stir-fry for another minute. Pour in the *dashi* and sake, bring to a boil, and simmer for 10 minutes.

Remove 2 tablespoons of stock from the wok and blend with the *miso* paste to dissolve it. Pour the mixture back into the wok and cook for another minute. Divide between 2 bowls.

*Fast and friendly service...
Delicious food... And the
waiters are a gorgeous
bunch of blokes, too!*
Anjin, Norway

roasted honey pork ramen

with seasonal greens, bamboo shoots, and barbecue sauce

Steaming broth, sweetened roasted pork, and lots of interesting greens to complete one of our popular specials. This dish is particularly sought after in the colder months, when big, gutsy flavors are required.

10 ounces pork fillet
2 tablespoons barbecue sauce (see page 29)
2 teaspoons honey
10 ounces *ramen* noodles
4 cups seasoned chicken stock (see page 17)
4 scallions, trimmed and cut into 1-inch lengths
2 handfuls of roughly chopped seasonal greens
12 pieces *menma* (canned bamboo shoots), drained

Preheat the oven to 425°F. Put the pork in a roasting tray, add the barbecue sauce, and toss to coat. Roast for about 30 minutes. After 25 minutes, pour the honey over it and return to the oven for the final 5 minutes. Let it rest for 5 minutes, then slice thinly.

Cook the noodles in a large pot of boiling water for 2–3 minutes until just tender. Drain thoroughly and divide between 2 bowls. In a saucepan, heat the chicken stock until boiling, add the scallions and greens, and cook for 30 seconds.

Ladle it over the noodles. Top with the *menma* and the pork.

When you order, your choice is keyed into an electronic pad, which sends the selection through to the kitchen. This means your food is often being prepared before you have even had time to settle down.

pork char siu men

five-spice roast pork with bok choy and noodles

11 ounces pork tenderloin

2 tablespoons vegetable oil

9 ounces *ramen* noodles

3 ounces pak choi or baby vegetables

4 cups chicken stock (see page 17)

12 pieces *menma* (canned bamboo shoots), drained

4 scallions, trimmed and chopped

for the marinade

1 tablespoon *char siu* sauce (see page 14)

½ teaspoon Chinese five spice (available from Oriental stores)

¼ teaspoon ground cinnamon

2 tablespoons sake

Put the pork and the marinade ingredients in a plastic freezer bag, seal and massage for a few minutes, then place in the fridge overnight or for as long as possible.

Preheat the oven to 300°F. Heat a heavy frying pan until hot, add the vegetable oil, and put the pork in for 2–3 minutes to seal, rolling it around until golden all over. Transfer to a roasting tray and roast for 50 minutes–1 hour. Remove and let it rest for 5 minutes, then slice on the diagonal.

Cook the noodles in a large pot of boiling water for 2–3 minutes or until just tender. Drain thoroughly and refresh under cold running water.

Steam or boil the bok choy for 1 minute (or vegetables for 5 minutes) until just tender. Put the stock in a pan and bring to a boil. Divide the noodles between 2 bowls and ladle over them the stock. Top with the slices of pork and bok choy, *menma,* and scallions.

tonkatsu

golden bread-crumbed pork with chile, daikon, and snow peas

The *katsu* dishes are popular sellers on the menu; it's something about those crispy bread crumbs. The recipe for *tonkatsu* comes from the Amsterdam wagamama where it has proved a popular dish from the day it appeared as a special.

2 carrots, peeled and cut into matchsticks

2 ounces *daikon* (mooli), peeled and cut into matchsticks

1 ounce snow peas, thinly sliced on the diagonal

8 scallions, trimmed and thinly sliced on the diagonal

1 green chile, trimmed, seeded, and sliced lengthwise

handful of bean sprouts, well rinsed

2 x 5-ounce pork loin steaks

flour, for dusting

1 egg, beaten

generous handful of *panko* bread crumbs (see page 15)

¼ cup vegetable oil

2 handfuls of salad greens

1 tablespoon tomato ketchup

2 tablespoons Worcestershire sauce

Put the carrots, *daikon*, snow peas, scallions, chile, and bean sprouts in iced water for 1 hour to crisp up. Drain thoroughly.

Place the pork between 2 sheets of plastic wrap and pound it with a rolling pin until only ¼-inch thick. Put the flour in one bowl, the egg in another, and the bread-crumbs in a third. Dip the pork first in the flour, then in the egg, and finally in the crumbs. Press gently to coat well.

Heat a heavy frying pan over medium heat for 1–2 minutes until hot and almost smoking and then add the oil. Add the pork and cook for 3 minutes on each side until golden. Drain the pork on paper towel and cut into ½-inch strips.

Divide between 2 plates, along with the drained vegetables, and arrange the salad greens alongside. Combine the ketchup and Worcestershire sauce and pour it around the pork.

lamb kare lomen

marinated lamb with soba noodles, cilantro, and teriyaki dipping sauce

7 ounces lamb fillet cutlets

2 garlic cloves, peeled, chopped, and mashed with a little salt

¼ cup vegetable oil

7 fluid ounces (a scant cup) *kare lomen* sauce (see page 38)

½ teaspoon salt

½ teaspoon sugar

½ teaspoon *dashi no moto* (see page 14)

7 fluid ounces (a scant cup) coconut milk

9 ounces thin white *somen* noodles

handful of bean sprouts

small bunch of cilantro (coriander leaves), roughly chopped

3 ounces cucumber, peeled and cut into matchsticks

for serving

1 tablespoon barbecue sauce (see page 29)

1 tablespoon teriyaki sauce, homemade (see page 28) or store-bought

2 lime wedges

Combine the lamb and garlic, toss well, and set aside.

Heat a wok over medium heat for 1–2 minutes or until completely hot and almost smoking and add the vegetable oil. Pour in the *kare lomen* sauce and simmer for 15 minutes, or until the sauce takes on a deep, dark red color and gives off a sweet, rounded aroma. Add a cup of water and bring to a boil, whisking all the time. Season with salt, sugar, and *dashi no moto*. Add the coconut milk and simmer for 5 minutes.

Preheat the broiler. Broil the lamb for 3 minutes, turn over, and repeat on the other side until cooked. Set aside in a warm place to rest.

Cook the noodles in a large pot of boiling water for 2–3 minutes or until just tender. Drain thoroughly, then divide between 2 bowls.

Spoon the hot *kare lomen* sauce over them and add the bean sprouts, cilantro, and cucumber. Top with the lamb, spoon over a little of the barbecue sauce and teriyaki sauce over it, and serve with the lime wedges.

zasai beef gohan

stir-fried beef with red pepper, mushrooms, oyster sauce, and rice

1 cup rice

2 tablespoons vegetable oil

5 ounces rump or sirloin steak, cut on the diagonal
  into thin strips

2 garlic cloves, peeled and mashed with a little salt

handful of snow peas, thinly sliced

4 scallions, trimmed and sliced

½ red pepper, trimmed, seeded, and cut into thin strips

8 baby corn, sliced

6 shiitake mushrooms, sliced

1 tablespoon *shaoshing* wine (see page 15)

pinch of salt

1 teaspoon white sugar

2 tablespoons light soy sauce

1 tablespoon oyster sauce

½ teaspoon cornstarch

1 tablespoon sesame oil

3 tablespoons *zasai* chili sauce (see page 36)

Cook the rice in a large pot of boiling water and drain. Heat a wok over medium heat for 1–2 minutes or until completely hot and almost smoking and add the vegetable oil. When it's hot, add the beef and garlic and stir-fry for 30 seconds. Then add the vegetables, wine, salt, sugar, soy sauce, oyster sauce, and ⅓ cup water.

Mix the cornstarch with 2 tablespoons of water and stir into the sauce. Bring to a boil, then stir in the sesame oil.

Divide the rice between 2 plates and top with the beef and vegetables, and the *zasai* chili sauce.

Simple food places a great deal of emphasis on finding the best ingredients; the freshest vegetables, well-aged meat, and mouthwatering sauces made alongside the main dish. Attention to detail drives all of what we do and this is equally important in a domestic kitchen.

7

vegetable
main dishes

On display in all wagamama kitchens is a chart simply headed "How To Cut." It lists all the vegetables we use and explains how to cut them. This level of detail is important for two reasons. First, as a restaurant group we must ensure consistency at a high standard. Second, how a dish looks is as essential to the Japanese as how it tastes and smells. Vision is, after all, one of our senses. So our team learns how to cut to ensure variety in a dish. Thus a pepper is cut in one of three ways—into chunks, sticks, or juliennes (matchsticks); a scallion is either thinly sliced or long-sliced; a carrot is shredded or cut into round slices.

There is, of course, another constraining factor: all the ingredients in the restaurant dishes (and in recipes here) can be eaten with chopsticks. That means they need to be cut into bite-sized and while this requirement limits the presentation, it also provides an enormously rewarding challenge.

Finding good vegetables is no easy task and at wagamama we face the same problems as the home cook, albeit on a different scale. We insist on the freshest bok choy, scallions, and salad greens. We go to great lengths to ensure our onions deliver punch without bitterness. We continuously strive to find cucumbers with crunch, carrots with bite, and mushrooms with flavor.

It is impossible to discuss vegetables in Japanese cooking and not raise the subject of tofu, an ingredient people in the West have been slow to adopt. Tofu is rich in protein, the main reason for its popularity in countries where protein sources were scarce (in Japan, for example, the eating of meat is relatively recent).

Put simply, tofu is the milk of soybeans, which is coagulated to make it solid—bean curd. It doesn't have a great deal of taste itself, but it readily absorbs the flavors of other stronger-tasting ingredients. In this it is not that different from modern chicken, which is quite mild-tasting and is often "improved" by being cooked with more strongly flavored ingredients.

the organic question Customers often ask about the relative merits of organic. Our answer remains the same: you must taste and judge for yourselves. In our experience, organic can sometimes be better, but it is not a universal truth. Rather than pinning our flag to the organic mast we prefer to go in search of what is best. That way we can ensure we deliver the maximum flavor and texture on the plate or in the bowl.

moyashi soba

stir-fried vegetables with sesame oil and soy sauce

9 ounces whole-wheat *ramen* noodles

4 cups vegetable stock (see page 18)

2 tablespoons vegetable oil

2 garlic cloves, peeled and crushed

2 large zucchinis, cut on the diagonal into ¼-inch thick slices

2 small leeks, trimmed and finely sliced

15 button mushrooms, finely sliced

14 sugarsnap peas

handful of bean sprouts

8 x 1-inch cubes of firm tofu

1 teaspoon salt

2 teaspoons sugar

2 tablespoons light soy sauce

2 teaspoons sesame oil

4 scallions, trimmed and cut into 1-inch-long slices

Cook the noodles in a large pot of boiling water for 2–3 minutes or until just tender. Drain, refresh under cold running water, and divide between 2 bowls. Bring the stock to a boil using the same pan and ladle it over the noodles.

Meanwhile, heat a wok over medium heat for 1–2 minutes or until completely hot and almost smoking, then add the vegetable oil. Stir-fry the garlic for 5 seconds, then add all the vegetables and tofu, but not the scallions. Stir-fry for 2–3 minutes until softened. Add the salt, sugar, and soy sauce, then drizzle the sesame oil over it. Divide between the bowls and top with the scallion slices.

noodles are delicious, quick, and easy. They are also a source of complex carbohydrates. *Soba* noodles, made from buckwheat, are particularly healthy, as buckwheat is said to thin the blood and is thought to be one explanation for the low rate of heart disease in Japan. A reason, if one is needed, to slurp away.

rice noodle soup

with grilled tofu steak, miso, and choy sum

5 ounces rice noodles

2 x 9-ounce blocks firm tofu, cut into 2 steaks

2 tablespoons *miso* paste (see page 19)

½ teaspoon *shichimi* (see page 15)

1 tablespoon vegetable oil

handful of roughly chopped choy sum (see page 14)

4 cups *miso* soup (see page 46) or vegetable stock (see page 18)

small handful of cilantro (coriander leaves)

Soak the noodles in hot water for 2 minutes, drain, refresh under cold running water, and divide between 2 bowls. Place the tofu steaks between sheets of paper towel, and pat dry. Combine the *miso* paste and *shichimi* and spread it over the top of each steak.

Heat a grill pan until hot and oil lightly with paper towel dipped in vegetable oil. Place the tofu on the grill pan, *miso*-side up, for 6–8 minutes or until the tofu is hot and the bottom is crispy. Remove the steaks and cook the choy sum on the grill pan until just wilted. Bring the *miso* soup or stock to a boil and ladle it over the noodles. Top with the choy sum and grilled tofu. Scatter with cilantro.

Shopping for noodles is nothing like as difficult as it once was. Most supermarkets now carry quite a range, although ethnic supermarkets tend to be more extensive both in terms of type and the brands they have. Is there much to tell between each brand? Not a great deal, the best idea is to try a few and find one you like.

yasai chili men

stir-fried chili vegetables with tofu and soba noodles

9 ounces *soba* noodles

2 tablespoons vegetable oil

6 x ¾-inch cubes, firm tofu

6 button mushrooms, sliced

handful of sugarsnap peas

1 zucchini, cut on the diagonal into ¼-inch slices

2 carrots, peeled and thinly sliced

2 tomatoes, quartered

1¼ cups chili sauce (see page 27)

Cook the noodles in a large pot of boiling water for 2–3 minutes or until just tender. Drain and refresh under cold running water. Heat a wok over medium heat for 1–2 minutes or until completely hot and almost smoking, then add the vegetable oil. Once it's hot, add the tofu and stir-fry for about 5 minutes until golden. Add all the vegetables and stir-fry for 3–4 minutes until they are tender. Pour in the chili sauce and bring to a boil. Divide the noodles between 2 plates and top with the stir-fry.

ginger chile mushrooms

with soba noodles, scallions, and cilantro

9 ounces *soba* noodles

3 tablespoons vegetable oil

1 red chile, trimmed, seeded, and finely sliced

2 tablespoons peeled and grated fresh ginger root

4 oyster mushrooms, cut into ½-inch slices

4 shiitake mushrooms, cut into ½-inch slices

clump of enoki mushrooms, about the size of your fist, broken up

handful of roughly chopped choy sum (see page 14)

½ teaspoon salt

1 teaspoon sugar

generous handful of bean sprouts

2½ cups *miso* soup (see page 46)

4 scallions, trimmed and sliced

2 sprigs of cilantro (coriander leaves)

Cook the noodles in a large pot of boiling water for 2–3 minutes or until just tender. Drain, refresh under cold running water, and divide between 2 bowls. Heat a wok over a medium heat for 1–2 minutes or until completely hot and almost smoking, then add the vegetable oil. Add the sliced red chile and grated ginger and stir-fry for 15–20 seconds, then add the oyster, shiitake, and enoki mushrooms along with the choy sum. Season with salt and sugar, and stir-fry for 2–3 minutes.

Put the bean sprouts on top of the noodles, spoon the mushrooms over them, then ladle over it the hot *miso* soup. Scatter with the scallion slices and cilantro.

You only stir-fry once, so everything has to be chopped to fit in with the time frame. This can seem a chore when you've been "cooking" for 20 minutes without turning the heat on, but it all happens in a flash at the end.

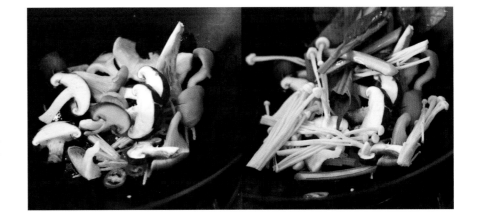

marinated vegetable ramen

with soy sauce, garlic, and chile

1 small eggplant, trimmed and sliced
vegetable oil
1 small sweet potato, peeled and sliced
4 medium mushrooms, cut in half
1 zucchini, sliced
4 baby corn, cut in half lengthwise
4 scallions, trimmed and cut into 1-inch slices
2 tablespoons light soy sauce
1 teaspoon finely chopped garlic
1 red chile, trimmed, seeded, and finely chopped
9 ounces whole-wheat *ramen* noodles
4 cups vegetable stock (see page 18)

Heat a grill pan until smoking. Brush the eggplant slices with oil. Put all the other vegetables in a large bowl and toss with 3 tablespoons of vegetable oil until everything is coated.

Grill the eggplant first, for 4 minutes on each side, or until tender. Then grill the sweet potato, mushrooms, and zucchini, all of which should take about 2–3 minutes on each side. Finally cook the corn and scallions for 1 minute on each side.

Transfer to a bowl, drizzle the soy sauce over it, add the garlic and chile, and toss, then cover with plastic wrap. (It is important to marinate the vegetables while they are hot so that they absorb the flavors. They will soften up more while cooling.) Set aside to marinate for at least 20 minutes.

Cook the noodles in a large pot of boiling water for 2–3 minutes or until just tender. Drain thoroughly and divide between 2 bowls. Bring the vegetable stock to a boil and check the vegetables; if they are still a little tough, cook in the stock until tender. Ladle the stock and vegetables over the noodles, and serve.

Charbroiled eggplant has a meatiness quite unlike any other vegetable; succulent, full-flavored, and packed with gutsy attitude. Who needs meat when a vegetable can deliver all this?

yasai korroke

vegetable patties with amai sauce, mixed greens, and wakame

makes 6 patties

1 large potato, peeled and cut into chunks

1 small sweet potato, peeled and cut into chunks

salt and white pepper

¼ cup frozen peas

¼ cup canned corn, drained

vegetable oil, for deep-frying

1 small onion, peeled and finely chopped

1 red chile, trimmed, seeded, and finely chopped

3–4 tablespoons plain flour

1 egg, beaten

1 heaping cup *panko* bread crumbs (see page 15)

2 tablespoons *amai* sauce (see page 22)

2 handfuls of salad greens

2 tablespoons wagamama salad dressing (see page 32)

½ red pepper, trimmed, seeded, and cut into thin strips

¼ cup *wakame* (see page 15), soaked in warm water for
   5 minutes, drained, and roughly chopped

Calling these vegetable patties doesn't really do them justice. Light, delicate, and remarkably full-flavored, they deliver quite a punch along with the amai sauce.

Put the potato and sweet potato in a pan of boiling salted water and cook for 10–12 minutes until tender. Add the peas for the last 2 minutes. Drain, return to the pan, then crush slightly with a wooden spoon to create a lumpy mash. Stir in the corn.

Heat 2 tablespoons of the oil in a frying pan and cook the onion and chile over a low heat for 6–8 minutes until soft. Combine the onion and chile with the cooked ingredients in a large bowl, season, and mix evenly. Let it cool, divide into 6 equal portions, and shape into flat patties.

Place the flour in a bowl, the beaten egg in another bowl, and the bread crumbs in a third. Dip each patty first in the flour, then in the egg and finally in the crumbs.

Fill a pan two-thirds full with oil and heat to 350°F, or until a cube of bread added to the oil browns in 30 seconds. Lower in the patties, 3 at a time, and deep-fry for 2–3 minutes until golden brown and crisp. Drain the patties on paper towels and keep warm while you deep-fry the rest.

Arrange the vegetable patties on 2 plates. Heat the *amai* sauce and drizzle it around the plate. Mix the salad greens with the dressing and place on top of the patties. Top with red pepper strips and *wakame*.

pumpkin curry

with tofu, brown rice, baby spinach, and coconut ginger sauce

3 tablespoons vegetable oil

1 small pumpkin, peeled, seeded, and cut into wedges

2 zucchini, cut into small chunks

6 button mushrooms, cut in half

4 baby corn

handful of sugarsnap peas

4 x 1-inch cubes of firm tofu

7 fluid ounces (a scant cup) coconut ginger sauce (see page 25)

½ cup brown rice

2 handfuls of baby spinach

handful of chopped cilantro (coriander leaves)

Heat a wok over medium heat for 1–2 minutes or until completely hot and almost smoking, then add the vegetable oil. Add the pumpkin, zucchini, mushrooms, baby corn, and sugarsnap peas, and stir-fry for 2 minutes. Add the tofu and the coconut ginger sauce, season with a little salt, and continue cooking for another 15–20 minutes, or until the pumpkin is tender. Cook the rice according to the instructions on the package. Drain, and divide between 2 plates. Scatter the baby spinach on the plate alongside and on top of the curry. Sprinkle with chopped cilantro.

this recipe comes from the Dublin wagamama where it was introduced as a special. Such was the response, it has kept reappearing as a special ever since. It is full-flavored and gutsy, a winter warmer to cheer you up and one for those summer days that are not quite as sunny as you might have hoped for. The dish takes a little longer to cook than most but the time involves everything simmering away gently so you can put your feet up and relax.

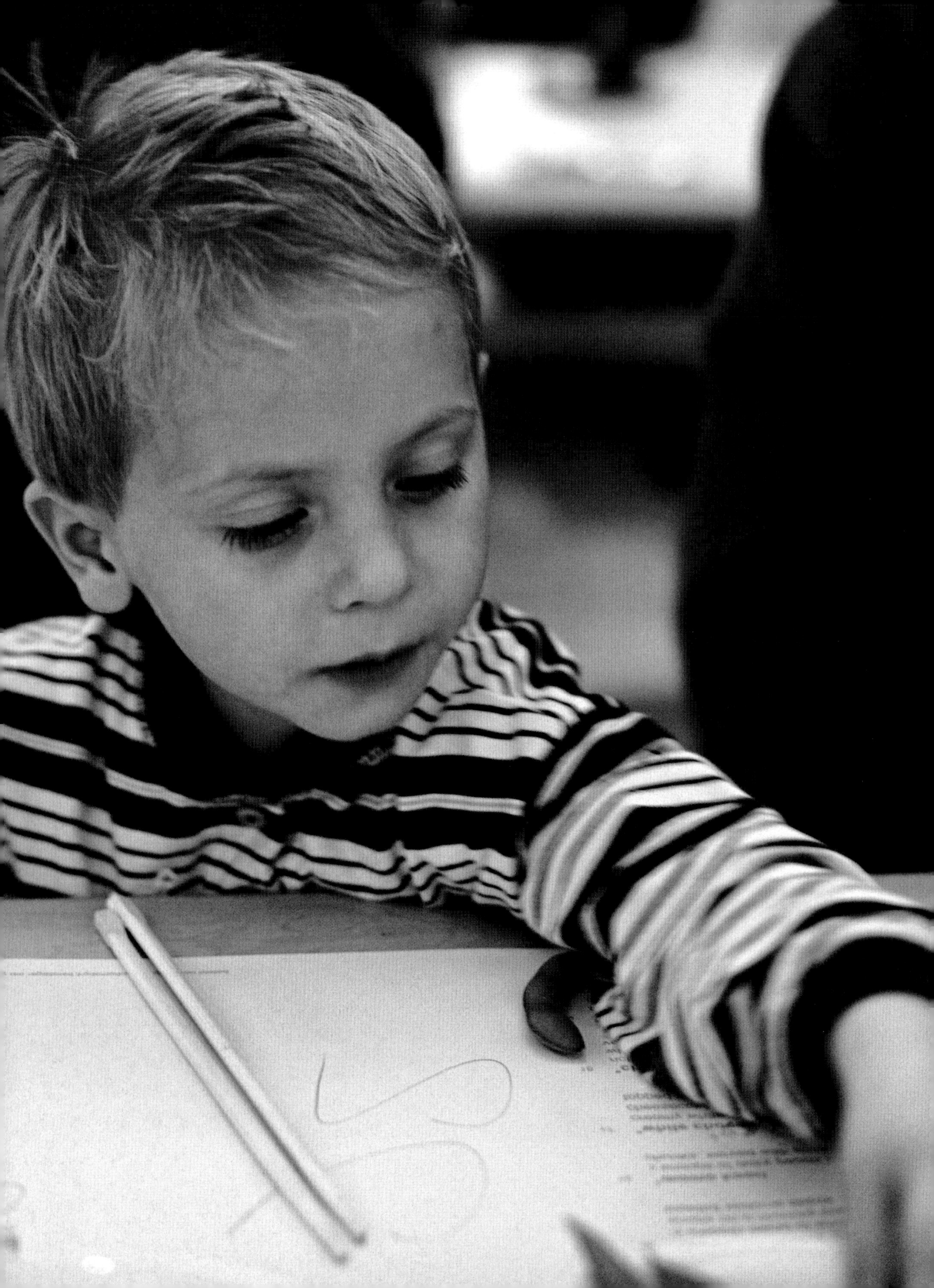

spiced vegetable stir-fry

with chile, soy sauce, miso soup, and lemongrass

3 tablespoons vegetable oil

1 garlic clove, peeled and sliced

1 red chile, trimmed, seeded, and sliced

1 lemongrass stalk, outer leaves removed, and sliced

1 red onion, peeled and chopped into ½-inch pieces

2 small leeks, cut on the diagonal into 1-inch lengths

12 snow peas

10 baby corn, cut in half lengthwise

handful of bean sprouts

4 bok choy, roughly chopped

pinch of salt

½ teaspoon sugar

2 tablespoons light soy sauce

9 ounces noodles

2½ cups *miso* soup (see page 46)

Heat a wok over medium heat for 1–2 minutes or until completely hot and almost smoking, then add the vegetable oil. Add the garlic, chile, and lemongrass and stir-fry for 30 seconds. Add the onion and leeks and stir-fry for another minute. Add the remaining vegetables and season with salt, sugar, and soy sauce. Stir-fry for another 3 minutes until all the vegetables are tender.

Cook the noodles in a large pot of boiling water for 2–3 minutes or until just tender. Drain thoroughly. Heat the *miso* soup in another pan. Divide the vegetables and noodles between 2 bowls and ladle the hot *miso* soup over them.

Previous pages: Happy staff mean happy customers. People, young and old and from all walks of life, enjoy the constant buzz and energy of the restaurants.

You don't need a wok in order to stir fry, but it certainly makes life a lot easier. They are not expensive pieces of kit, particularly if you source one from an ethnic store.

yasai cha han

stir-fried vegetable rice with soy sauce, miso soup, and pickled vegetables

¾ cup Thai fragrant rice
¼ cup vegetable oil
14 button mushrooms, quartered
¾-inch cubes of firm tofu
handful of baby corn
handful of sugarsnap peas
4 scallions, trimmed and cut into 1½-inch lengths
1 teaspoon salt
3 tablespoons light soy sauce
2 eggs, beaten
for serving
miso soup (see page 46)
¼ cup Oriental pickled (or preserved) vegetables (see page 15)

Cook the rice in a large pan of boiling water until tender. Drain, refresh under cold running water, and set aside.

Heat a wok over medium heat for 1–2 minutes or until completely hot and almost smoking, then add the vegetable oil. Add the mushrooms and stir-fry for 2 minutes. Add the tofu and continue stir-frying for 3 more minutes, or until lightly colored. Add the corn, sugarsnap peas, and scallions, and stir-fry over medium heat until all the ingredients are warmed through. Add the rice, season with salt and soy sauce, and stir-fry for another 2 minutes.

Add the eggs and stir-fry vigorously until they are just cooked. Divide the stir-fry mixture between 2 bowls. Heat the *miso* soup and serve separately, with the pickled vegetables on the side.

yasai dotenabe

stir-fried vegetables and tofu with ginger, sesame oil, and miso

7 ounces *udon* noodles

¼ cup vegetable oil

7 ounces firm tofu, cut into 1-inch cubes

2 garlic cloves, peeled and crushed

1 tablespoon peeled and grated fresh ginger root

14 chestnut mushrooms, thickly sliced

½ red pepper, trimmed, seeded, and cut into strips

1 bok choy, trimmed, washed and quartered

1 small leek, trimmed and cut into strips

½ small carrot, peeled and cut into strips

1 teaspoon salt

1 teaspoon sugar

2 teaspoons light soy sauce

2 tablespoons sesame oil

2½ cups *miso* soup (see page 46)

few sprigs of cilantro (coriander leaves)

12 pieces *menma* (canned bamboo shoots), drained

Cook the noodles in a large pot of boiling water for 2–3 minutes or until just tender. Drain and refresh under cold running water.

Heat a wok over medium heat for 1–2 minutes or until completely hot and almost smoking, then add the vegetable oil. Add the tofu and stir-fry for 4–5 minutes until golden. Add the garlic and ginger and stir-fry without letting them color for about 10 seconds. Add the mushrooms, red pepper, bok choy, leek, and carrot, and stir-fry for 3 minutes until tender. Season with the salt, sugar, soy sauce, and sesame oil, and toss well.

Heat the *miso* soup. Divide the noodles and stir-fry between 2 bowls and ladle the hot soup over them. Top with the cilantro and *menma*.

yasai yaki soba

stir-fried vegetables with eggs, soba noodles, and sesame seeds

9 ounces *soba* noodles

2 eggs

½ green pepper, trimmed, seeded, and cut into strips

½ red pepper, trimmed, seeded, and cut into strips

1 onion, peeled and thinly sliced

8 scallions, trimmed and sliced

2 ounces button mushrooms, sliced

2 garlic cloves, peeled and finely chopped

handful of bean sprouts

2 tablespoons *yaki soba* sauce (see page 32)

3 tablespoons vegetable oil

2 teaspoons pickled ginger (*gari*, see page 14)

1 tablespoon dried shallots

½ teaspoon sesame seeds

2 tablespoons *yasai soba* dressing (see page 39)

Cook the noodles in a large pot of boiling water for 2–3 minutes or until tender. Drain and refresh under cold running water. Beat the eggs in a bowl and add all the vegetables and the *yaki soba* sauce.

Heat a wok over medium heat for 1–2 minutes or until completely hot and almost smoking, then add the vegetable oil. Add the egg mixture and the cooked noodles, and stir-fry for 3 minutes. Divide between 2 bowls and top with the pickled ginger, shallots, sesame seeds, and dressing.

noodles are cooked in exactly the same way as pasta; lots of boiling water. But because the noodles are already salted, there is no need to salt the water, just make sure it is properly boiling.

yasai itameru

stir-fried tofu with mixed vegetables, rice noodles, and coconut ginger sauce

5 ounces rice noodles

3 tablespoons vegetable oil

1 tablespoon garlic paste (homemade or store-bought)

1 red chile, trimmed, seeded, and finely chopped

7 ounces firm tofu, cut into 1-inch cubes

3 bok choy, cut in half lengthwise

1 red onion, peeled and thickly sliced

5 scallions, trimmed and cut into 1-inch lengths

1 small sweet potato, peeled and cut into matchsticks

2 handfuls of bean sprouts

1 teaspoon salt

1 teaspoon sugar

2 tablespoons light soy sauce

1 teaspoon sesame oil

9 fluid ounces coconut ginger sauce (see page 25)

12 cilantro (coriander leaf) sprigs

1 lime, cut into slices

Cook the noodles in a large pot of boiling water for 2–3 minutes or until tender. Drain and refresh under cold running water.

Heat a wok over medium heat for 1–2 minutes or until completely hot and almost smoking, then add the vegetable oil. Stir in the garlic paste and red chile, cook for 10 seconds, then add the tofu, bok choy, red onion, scallions, sweet potato, and bean sprouts, and stir-fry for about 5 minutes.

Add the salt, sugar, and soy sauce, and stir-fry for 4–5 minutes until the vegetables are tender. Remove from the heat, drizzle the sesame oil over it, and stir to combine.

In a separate pan, mix the coconut ginger sauce into the noodles and warm them through over a low heat. Divide between 2 plates and top with the stir-fry mixture, cilantro, and lime slices.

For years, people in the West have tended to view tofu as a sort of non-food. Although it lacks much flavor on its own, it is full of protein and is a great team player, liking nothing more than soaking up lots of gutsy flavors.

8
salads

What makes a good salad? For many it is the dressing and for years we have resisted repeated requests to reveal our recipe. No longer: it is given on page 32.

There is, however, rather more to a good salad than the dressing. A salad must provide variety, but it must also have direction, a focus, that ensures it does not become simply a basket for everything.

Popular consensus seems to demand greens of some description. Loosely this means lettuce, but rather more unusual greens—like arugula and mizuna—also come into this category. Varying the greens is one way to change a salad and allow it to evolve—more watercress and corn salad (mâche) in winter perhaps; maybe greater use of Bibb (limestone) lettuce in summer.

Some of our salads use noodles and this picks up on the popular Japanese custom of eating cold *soba* noodles with a soy dipping sauce: comforting food to be enjoyed for its simplicity.

Defining what makes a salad a salad and a dish a dish is no easy task, particularly when you include warm salads. Most are eaten cold, however, and the idea is that all the ingredients are dressed. In Japanese cuisine, dressed salads are called *aemono* and they make up one of the cooking styles used in a meal—the others being deep-fried (*agemono*), grilled (*yakimono*), sautéed (*itammono*), simmered (*nimono*), steamed (*mushimono*), and vinegared (*sunomono*).

How these different techniques are used enables the all-important balance to come into play. Not too much of any one thing, which even in a feast is important. Salads aim to refresh, to provide relief from the more complex and heavier dishes. Yet modern habits have meant they are now almost a meal in themselves.

In the summer months particularly, customers often have a salad and nothing else; a light and refreshing break from a hectic schedule. There is something very welcoming about a plate of colorful leaves with lots of other elements dotted about. Freshness is everything in a salad; crisp leaves, crunchy bean sprouts, and freshly cooked noodles all dressed with the heady delights of ginger, soy, and sesame, cilantro (coriander leaves), *miso*, and lime juice.

asparagus and green-tea noodle salad

with red pepper, chile, and cilantro

2½–3½-inch piece of *daikon* (mooli), peeled

1 small carrot, peeled

2 ounces *soba* noodles, cooked for 2–3 minutes in 1 cup
    boiling green tea and refreshed under cold running water

3 ounces buckwheat noodles, cooked for 2–3 minutes in
    boiling water and refreshed under cold running water

½ red pepper, trimmed, seeded, and cut into strips

1 red chile, trimmed, seeded, and sliced

¾ ounce *kombu* (see page 14), soaked in cold water, squeezed dry,
    and cut into thin strips

2–3 tablespoons wagamama salad dressing (see page 32)

salt

1 small bunch of asparagus, spears cut in half lengthwise

2 handfuls of bean sprouts

1 tablespoon vegetable oil

handful of roughly chopped choy sum (see page 14)

small bunch of cilantro (coriander leaves), roughly chopped

Shred the *daikon* and carrot. (This is best done with a food mill or in a food processor to give you fine strands.) Place the *daikon* and carrot in a bowl of water with several ice cubes and place in the fridge for 1 hour to crisp up. Drain well, mix together with the noodles, red pepper, red chile, *kombu,* and salad dressing, and season with salt. Divide between 2 plates.

Heat a grill pan until smoking and toss the asparagus and bean sprouts in the oil and a seasoning of salt. Cook on the grill pan for 2–3 minutes, turning occasionally, until lightly charred. Add the choy sum towards the end so that it just wilts. Let it cool, add to the rest of the salad, and top with the cilantro.

grilled tofu steak salad

with noodles, scallions, and sake

9 ounces firm tofu, cut into 2 steaks about ¾-inch thick,
   each steak cut into 6 squares
¼ cup sake
2 tablespoons light soy sauce
2 teaspoons sesame oil
1 garlic clove, peeled and crushed
1 teaspoon peeled and grated fresh ginger root
salt
4 scallions, sliced at an angle
a little vegetable oil
2 handfuls of salad greens
3 tablespoons wagamama salad dressing (see page 32)
¼ cucumber, seeds removed and finely shredded
large handful of bean sprouts, blanched for 10 seconds and
   refreshed under cold water
½ lime, sliced

Charbroiling is not difficult, but it does require confidence. Move your ingredients too quickly and you will soon discover they have stuck to the surface. Leave them alone for long enough and they have a way of unsticking, as if by magic.

Place the tofu on a clean lint-free dishtowel, cover with another clean towel, and place 2 cutting boards on top to press lightly. Leave for at least 30 minutes.

Combine the sake, soy sauce, sesame oil, garlic, ginger, and salt to taste in a bowl, then add the tofu. Scatter the scallions over it and let it marinate for 45 minutes, tossing occasionally. Remove the tofu from the marinade, shaking off the scallions, and reserving the excess marinade.

Heat a grill pan until smoking and lightly oil it with some paper towel dipped in vegetable oil. Place the tofu on the grill pan and cook for 2–3 minutes on each side until golden brown, then set aside. In a bowl, toss the salad greens in the salad dressing and place on the side of 2 plates.

Mix together the cucumber and blanched bean sprouts and place alongside the salad greens, topped with the lime slices. Arrange the tofu steaks around the salad and spoon the reserved marinade over them.

rice noodle salad

with sweet potato, butternut squash, red pepper, and sweet miso

1 small sweet potato, peeled and cut into ¾-inch chunks

1 red pepper, trimmed, seeded, and thinly sliced

½ small butternut squash, peeled, seeded, and cut into ¾-inch chunks

2 tablespoons vegetable oil

salt

6 ounces dried rice sticks, soaked in boiling water for 5 minutes or until tender

1 tablespoon chile and cilantro dressing (see page 22)

handful of snow peas, sliced on the diagonal

4 shiitake mushrooms, sliced

generous handful of bean sprouts

3 tablespoons sweet *miso* dressing (see page 35)

2 sprigs of cilantro (coriander leaves)

Preheat the oven to 400°F. Put the sweet potato, red pepper, and butternut squash in a roasting pan, toss with the oil, and season with salt. Roast for 20 minutes or until tender and then let cool.

   Put all the ingredients except the cilantro in a large bowl and toss. Pile into 2 bowls and top with the cilantro.

smoked salmon salad

with egg noodles, scallions, and apricots

1 ¼ cups green tea

5 ounces dried egg noodles

2 slices (3 ounces) smoked salmon, cut into ⅛-inch strips

½ red pepper, seeded and cut into sticks

1 small red onion, peeled and thinly sliced

6 scallions, trimmed and sliced on the diagonal

1 red chile, trimmed, seeded, and thinly sliced

generous handful of bean sprouts

6 ready-to-eat dried apricots, thinly sliced

2 tablespoons light soy sauce

2 tablespoons vegetable oil

2 teaspoons chili sauce (see page 27)

few sprigs of cilantro (coriander leaves)

Strain the tea into a saucepan and bring to a boil. Add the noodles, turn off the heat, and leave for 5 minutes or until tender. Drain well, refresh briefly under cold running water, and set aside.

Combine the salmon, red pepper, red onion, scallions, chile, bean sprouts, and dried apricots in a large bowl. Stir the soy sauce and oil through them, add the noodles, and stir again. Divide between 2 plates and top with the chili sauce and cilantro.

Behind the casual, relaxed atmosphere of the restaurants there is a systemized approach aimed at ensuring customers experience the best service consistently. Feedback is encouraged and staff involvement is an integral part of the job. We believe in the whole idea of little improvements often. It allows us to evolve and develop.

salmon salad

charbroiled salmon with zucchini, peppers, cherry tomatoes, and cucumber

Seared salmon is a winner every time; crisp, salty skin, and underneath, rich, full-flavored flesh. Cooking is easy, too, as the fish turns opaque before your very eyes.

2 zucchinis, sliced

a little vegetable oil

salt

2 x 6-ounce salmon fillets

6 cherry tomatoes

½ cucumber, cut into strips

1 small carrot, peeled and cut into strips

½ red pepper, trimmed, seeded, and cut into strips

½ yellow pepper, trimmed, seeded, and cut into strips

6 tablespoons cucumber dressing (see page 26)

2 handfuls of mixed salad greens

small handful of cilantro (coriander leaves)

1 lemon, cut into wedges

Heat a grill pan until really hot. Lightly oil the zucchini slices and spread them on the grill pan in a single layer. Cook for 3 minutes on each side without disturbing. Transfer to a bowl and season with salt. Oil the salmon and cook for 4 minutes on each side, starting skin-side down, until opaque right through. Let it cool.

Mix all the vegetables together with half the dressing and divide between 2 plates. Put the salad greens on the side. Top with the salmon and cilantro, and drizzle the rest of the dressing around the plate. Serve with a lemon wedge.

ginger chicken salad

with red pepper, scallions, and lime

Chicken breast is often used in restaurants even though it has a tendency toward dryness. Thigh and leg meat, although darker, tends to be much more succulent and rich and often has more flavor. Both are interchangeable, but I know which one most chefs would favor.

vegetable oil, for deep frying

7 ounces boneless, skinless chicken thigh meat, cubed, and marinated overnight in chile and cilantro dressing (see page 22)

4 tablespoons cornstarch

2 handfuls of mixed salad leaves

¼ cup wagamama salad dressing (see page 32)

4 scallions, trimmed and finely sliced on the diagonal

1 red pepper, seeded and cut into matchsticks

1 lime, cut in half

Pour enough oil into a heavy pan to come two thirds of the way up the sides. Place it over a medium heat and heat it until the oil reaches 350°F or until a cube of bread added to the oil browns in 30 seconds.

Remove the chicken from the marinade, shaking off any excess. Put the cornstarch on a plate and dip the chicken in it to coat (or toss both in a plastic bag).

Lower the chicken into the oil and deep-fry for 3–4 minutes or until golden and cooked through.

Divide the salad greens between 2 plates and place the chicken in the center. Pour the dressing over it. Top with the scallions and red pepper, and serve with a lime half.

Deep-frying is about the oil and the temperature. You need fresh, pure vegetable oil and the correct heat. Too cool and whatever you are cooking absorbs the oil. Too hot and the outside cooks before the inside has had a chance to blink.

tamarind chicken salad

with red onion, ginger, and amai sauce

1 tablespoon vegetable oil

1 red onion, peeled and cut into chunks

2 boneless, skinless chicken breasts, cut into strips and marinated
   overnight in chile and cilantro dressing (see page 22)

generous handful of bean sprouts

2 handfuls of mixed salad greens

3 tablespoons wagamama salad dressing (see page 32)

1-inch piece of fresh ginger root, peeled and grated

3 tablespoons *amai* sauce (see page 22)

½ cucumber, shredded

small handful of roughly chopped cilantro (coriander leaves)

Heat a wok or large frying pan over medium heat for 1–2 minutes or until completely hot and almost smoking, then add the vegetable oil. Add the red onion and stir-fry over a low-medium heat for 5 minutes until lightly caramelized.

Increase the heat and add the chicken, stir-fry for 1 minute, and then add the bean sprouts. Stir-fry for 2–3 minutes to finish cooking.

In a bowl, toss the salad greens in the dressing and then divide between 2 plates. Place the chicken stir-fry in the center. In a small bowl or cup, combine the grated ginger and *amai* sauce, spoon it over the chicken, and top with the shredded cucumber and cilantro.

It may be the ramen dishes you are famous for, but for me it's the salads that really get me going!
Mark, Perth

warm stir-fried chicken salad

marinated chicken with lime, chile, cilantro, and toasted sesame seeds

4 boneless, skinless chicken thighs, cut into strips
3 tablespoons vegetable oil
for the marinade
1 teaspoon sesame oil
2 garlic cloves, peeled and crushed
2 teaspoons fish sauce (see page 14)
2 teaspoons light soy sauce
juice of 1 lime
2 teaspoons ground cumin
1 large red chile, trimmed and chopped
2 teaspoons toasted sesame seeds (see below)
for the salad
2 handfuls of mixed salad greens
2 tablespoons wagamama salad dressing (see page 32)
2 teaspoons toasted sesame seeds (see below)
1 tablespoon chopped cilantro (coriander leaves)
1 lime, cut in half

Put all the ingredients for the marinade except the sesame seeds in a blender and blend until smooth, then stir in the sesame seeds. Put the chicken into a dish, pour the marinade over it, cover with plastic wrap, and marinate for at least 2 hours (overnight if possible) in the fridge.

Heat a wok over medium heat for 1–2 minutes or until completely hot and almost smoking, then add the vegetable oil. Add the chicken, stirring constantly so the pieces cook evenly, and stir-fry for 4–5 minutes until caramelized around the edges and cooked through.

In a bowl, mix the salad greens with the dressing. Divide it between 2 plates and scatter the toasted sesame seeds and chopped cilantro over it. Top with the chicken and serve with a lime half on each plate.

to toast sesame seeds, heat a dry frying pan and when hot, add the seeds, tossing the pan so they are evenly colored. Have a plate standing by to tip them onto or they are likely to burn.

spiced chicken salad

with star anise, sake, soy sauce, and red pepper

7 ounces boneless, skinless chicken thigh meat,
   cut into 1-inch cubes
1-inch piece of fresh ginger root, peeled and finely grated
1 lemongrass stalk, outer leaves removed, finely sliced
2 garlic cloves, peeled, chopped, and mashed with a little salt
1 red chile, trimmed, seeded, and finely chopped
2 star anise
2 tablespoons sake
2 tablespoons light soy sauce
¼ cup cornstarch
vegetable oil, for frying

for the salad

2 large handfuls of mixed salad leaves
4 spring onions, trimmed and finely sliced
1 red pepper, trimmed, seeded, and thinly sliced
2 tablespoons wagamama salad dressing (see page 32)
juice and zest of 1 lime

Put the chicken in a dish and scatter the ginger, lemongrass, garlic, chile, star anise, sake, and soy sauce over it. Using your hands, turn everything gently for a few minutes. Cover with plastic wrap and marinate for at least 1 hour, and overnight if possible, in the fridge.

Remove the chicken from the marinade, shaking off any excess. Put the cornstarch in a bowl and dip the chicken in to coat. Heat a large frying pan with ¾ inch of oil. Add the chicken and pan-fry for 8 minutes, turning occasionally.

Divide the salad greens between 2 plates and top with the chicken. Scatter the scallions and red pepper around it. Combine the salad dressing with the juice and zest of the lime and drizzle it over the top.

we marinate a lot of meat in the restaurants. This is done by combining the meat and the marinade in a plastic bag and gently massaging it. The same principle works well at home, too. Simply dropping the meat into the marinade is not enough; you have to work the two together to get an exchange of flavors.

beef itameru

marinated beef stir-fry with red onion, dressed salad greens, and amai sauce

11 ounces sirloin steak, trimmed and cut into thin strips

2 tablespoons chile and cilantro dressing (see page 22)

3 tablespoons vegetable oil

1 small red onion, peeled and cut into chunks

2 handfuls of bean sprouts

2 large handfuls of mixed peppery salad greens

2 tablespoons wagamama salad dressing (see page 32)

2 teaspoons peeled and grated fresh ginger root

3 tablespoons *amai* sauce (see page 22)

¼ cucumber, seeded and cut into thin strips

small bunch of cilantro (coriander leaves), roughly chopped

Combine the beef and chile and cilantro dressing and toss so the meat is well coated. Cover with plastic wrap and marinate for at least 1 hour, and overnight if possible, in the fridge.

Heat a wok or large, heavy frying pan over medium heat for 1–2 minutes or until completely hot and almost smoking, then add the vegetable oil. Add the onion and stir-fry for 2 minutes until soft. Increase the heat to high and cook for 2 more minutes until lightly caramelized. Add the beef and stir-fry for 1–2 minutes or until lightly golden. Tip in the bean sprouts and cook for 2–3 minutes, then remove from the heat.

Place the salad greens in a large bowl and drizzle the salad dressing over them. Toss until all the greens are coated, then divide between 2 plates. Combine the ginger and *amai* sauce. Pile the beef up in the center of the plates and pour the sauce over it. Top with the cucumber and cilantro.

All our kitchens are open plan. The transparency means the chefs get to see how and what customers are eating and customers have full view of all the activity in the kitchen. This is a key part of the wagamama concept and it allows food to be prepared and delivered quickly.

hot beef salad

with chile, crab salad, and soy sauce

3 tablespoons vegetable oil

1 red onion, peeled and cut into half-moon slices

4 ounces broccoli florets or zucchini, cut into bite-sized pieces

9 ounces sirloin or rump steak, cut into thin strips

handful of snow peas, thinly sliced lengthwise

2 garlic cloves, peeled and crushed

1 red chile, trimmed, seeded, and sliced

1 crabstick, shredded (optional)

5 ounces bean sprouts

1 teaspoon sugar

1 teaspoon salt

1 tablespoon light soy sauce

1 lime, cut in half

2 tablespoons fried shallots (available from Oriental stores)

4 sprigs of cilantro (coriander leaves)

Heat a wok over medium heat for 1–2 minutes or until completely hot and almost smoking, then add the vegetable oil. Add the red onion and broccoli and stir-fry for 2–3 minutes until lightly browned. Add the beef and stir-fry for about 5 minutes until lightly browned. Add the snow peas, garlic, chile, crabstick, and bean sprouts and stir-fry for another 2–3 minutes. Add the sugar, salt, and soy sauce, and toss quickly. Divide between 2 plates, squeeze the juice from the lime over it and sprinkle with the shallots and cilantro.

Your salads have made me completely re-invent what I eat during the summer months. All that color and crunch leaves me feeling totally satisfied. I can hardly bear to look at a sandwich these days!
Helena, Western Australia

9
desserts

Most of these desserts are based on fruit, a reflection in part of the Japanese tendency to end a meal with fruit. There are many reasons for this, not least the long-standing aversion to dairy products and the fact that most Japanese homes do not have an oven, so baking is not a traditional activity.

We also concentrate on fruit as it is a healthy and light option to end a meal. The sense of well-being is central to the whole philosophy of wagamama: eat well and live well. So we charbroil fruit, infuse coconut into the odd creamy concoction—no need to be healthy all the time!—and gently poach pears in sake with spices for extra interest.

We have deliberately kept this chapter short. While confectionary in Japan is a very big—and sweet—part of the national cuisine, the more normal route to finish a meal is with carefully cut fruit, maybe with the benefit of a spice or two for added zest. This is what we do with papaya, for example, but the recipe will work equally well with mango, peaches, and nectarines when they are in season.

As with vegetables, the cutting, in terms of size as well as shape, is a very important part of the preparation. A bowl of whole fruit placed in the middle of the table for dessert is not as tempting to break into as a large plate of fruit which has been cut and fashioned enticingly. This is not to say the fruit display has to be intricate or formal, but a variety of shapes lends interest and if you and your guests are eating with chopsticks, it allows you to have one large plate in the center, and people can then pick as they like.

For those of you who desire something more substantial, we have added in some cooked desserts: fruit *katsu* is one, which is a variety of fruit dipped in bread crumbs and then briefly deep-fried. The green tea drizzle cake is another. Our customers get through an awful lot of green tea and one of our chefs came up with the idea of using this rather unique flavor in a cake. It tastes delicious served with a spoonful of crème fraîche or sour cream.

The perfect partner for these desserts is, of course, ice cream, hardly traditional but tasty nonetheless. Which only goes to reinforce the idea that while wagamama has its origins in Japan, it is quite unique, a combination of numerous different influences and aspects, something which is altogether rather more a sum than a collection of parts. Ice cream, anyone?

lemongrass and chile crème caramel

with sake and star anise

1 cup milk
2 lemongrass stalks, outer leaves removed, slightly bashed
1 dried red chile
2 tablespoons sake
1 cinnamon stick
1 star anise
¼ cup white sugar
1 egg and 2 yolks
2 x 5-ounce ramekins or custard cups

for the caramel

¼ cup water
¼ cup white sugar

Put the milk, lemongrass, chile, sake, cinnamon stick, and star anise in a pan and place over a low heat for 15 minutes, without letting it come to a boil. Turn off the heat and let it infuse.

Preheat the oven to 300°F. First prepare the caramel. Put the water and the sugar in a small pan over a very low heat, without letting it boil, until dissolved. Turn up the heat and boil until golden. Carefully pour into the bottom of the ramekins.

Whisk the sugar, egg, and yolks in a mixing bowl until light. Strain the infused milk onto the eggs, mix well, and pour this over the caramel. Place the ramekins in a roasting pan on the middle shelf of the oven, then fill the pan with enough boiling water to reach halfway up the sides of the ramekins. Bake for 40–45 minutes until set, still with a slight wobble, but not colored. Let them cool completely in the roasting pan. Invert onto 2 plates and serve.

introducing rice to a crème brulée (right) may seem like sacrilege to some yet the inherent creaminess of the rice works wonders both for flavor and texture. You can play around with other rices too, Italian arborio produces a richer, more rounded result and basmati has its fans.

coconut rice brulée

with cinnamon

2 tablespoons Japanese rice

1 cup coconut milk

¼ cup water

1 cinnamon stick

3 egg yolks

¼ cup white sugar

¼ cup heavy cream

1½ tablespoons demerara sugar, for glazing

2 x 5-ounce ramekins or custard cups

Preheat the oven to 300°F. Put the rice, half the coconut milk, the water, and cinnamon in a pan and bring to a boil. Simmer gently for 15 minutes, covered, stirring occasionally to prevent sticking. Turn off the heat and let stand, covered, for another 10 minutes until the rice is tender and the liquid has been absorbed. Divide between the 2 ramekins. Whisk the egg yolks with the white sugar until light.

Heat the cream and the remaining coconut milk in a small pan and whisk into the egg and sugar mixture. Stir to combine, then pour it over the rice. Place the ramekins in a roasting pan on the middle shelf of the oven, then fill the pan with enough boiling water to reach halfway up the sides of the ramekins. Bake for 45 minutes until almost set (there should still be a slight wobble). Remove from the oven and let them cool completely in the roasting pan. To serve, sprinkle the top with demerera sugar and *brulée* it, either using a blow torch or under a very hot broiler, until golden and crispy.

The essence of a good brulée lies in the just-set custard and a thin crust that yields to a little pressure. The ideal route, although risky, is to up-end the ramekin once you have dusted the sugar so only a fine coating is left. Trouble is, this can lead to custard on the floor!

fresh papaya

with chile, ginger, and lime

8 ounces papaya peeled, seeded, and cut widthwise into
   ¼-inch slices
1-inch piece of fresh ginger root, peeled and cut into thin strips
½ red chile, trimmed, seeded, and finely chopped
1 lime, quartered, for serving

Arrange the papaya on 2 plates. Scatter the ginger strips and the chopped chile on top. Serve with the lime wedges for squeezing over them.

fruit katsu

golden fruit with ice cream and mint

1 tablespoon *shichimi* flour (see page 19)

1 egg, beaten

5½ cups coconut *panko* bread crumbs (see page 19)

2 x ¼-inch slices of fresh pineapple, peeled and cored

1 banana, peeled and cut into 1½-inch slices

1 apple, peeled, cored, and cut into wedges

vegetable oil, for deep frying

for serving

vanilla ice cream

sprigs of mint

Place the *shichimi* flour in a bowl, the beaten egg in another, and the bread crumbs in a third. Dip the fruit first in the flour, then the egg, and finally the bread crumbs.

Fill a pan one-third full of oil and heat it to 350°F or until a cube of bread added to the oil browns in 30 seconds. Deep-fry the fruit in batches until golden brown. Remove from the oil and drain well on paper towels.

To serve, divide the fruit between 2 bowls and top with a scoop of ice cream and a sprig of fresh mint.

There aren't many restaurants where kids are encouraged to draw all over the placemats! My own two grab the crayons, order cha han or yaki soba and a drink, and settle in. They both seem to pick up on the buzz and the friend-liness of the staff. It's become part of their lives and will continue to be for some time probably.

banana katsu

with ice cream, red currants, and mint

1 tablespoon flour
1 egg, beaten
3 tablespoons *panko* bread crumbs
2 large bananas, peeled but left whole
vegetable oil, for deep-frying
confectioners' sugar, for dusting
4 scoops of vanilla ice cream, for serving

for decorating
few sprigs of red currants
sprigs of mint

Place the flour in a bowl, the beaten egg in another, and the bread crumbs in a third. Dip the bananas first in the flour, then in the egg, and finally in the bread crumbs until coated. Pour 2 inches of the vegetable oil in a pan and heat it to 350°F, or until a cube of bread added to the oil browns in 30 seconds.

Deep-fry the bananas for 3–4 minutes or until golden brown. Remove carefully with a slotted spoon, drain on paper towels, and dust with confectioners' sugar.

Divide between 2 plates and serve with the ice cream. Decorate with some red currants and mint.

The bread crumbs are key here—Japanese really are the best—but so, too, is the oil and its temperature. Use a pure vegetable oil every time and ensure it is hot enough or you'll end up absorbing too much of the oil into the bread crumbs.

charbroiled pineapple

and coconut broth

1 ³/₄ cups canned coconut milk
¹/₃ cup white sugar
juice of 1 lime and zest of ¹/₂ lime
2-inch piece of lemongrass stalk, outer leaves removed, sliced
4 x ¹/₂-inch slices of fresh pineapple, peeled and cored
   (or use canned pineapple rings)

Put the coconut milk, two thirds of the sugar, the lime juice and zest, and lemon-grass in a heavy pan over medium heat and simmer gently for 5 minutes. Remove and set aside to infuse and cool.

Heat a grill pan over a high heat until almost smoking. Sprinkle the remaining sugar over the pineapple slices. When the pan is hot, cook the pineapple for 1 minute on each side. Strain the broth, reheat gently, pour into 2 bowls, and add the pine-apple rings.

marinated mango

with coconut sherbet

¹/₂ cup white sugar
¹/₂ cup water
1 ounce fresh ginger root, peeled and grated
1 star anise
juice and zest of 1 lime
1 ripe mango, peeled, pitted, and cut into ¹/₄-inch slices
2 scoops of coconut or lime sherbet, for serving

Put the sugar, water, ginger, star anise, lime juice and zest in a pan over medium heat until the sugar is dissolved. Increase the heat and simmer for 15 minutes until fragrant and syrupy, but still clear. Set aside to cool.

When cool, add the sliced mango and let it marinate overnight in the fridge. Fan the slices of mango in a circle in the center of a serving plate, spoon some of the syrup over them, and serve with a scoop of sherbet.

spiced fruit compote

with sake

1 cup water

½ cup white sugar

2 star anise

1 cinnamon stick

1 dried red chile

2 oranges (you need the zest of 1 and the juice of 2)

1 apple, peeled, cored, and cut into ½-inch cubes

1 Chinese pear, peeled, cored and cut into ½-inch cubes

12 dried apricots

2 ounces dried banana

2 ounces dried papaya

2 ounces dried mango

12 lychees, peeled, pitted, and cut in half

⅓ cup sake

Put the water, sugar, star anise, cinnamon, chile, orange juice and zest in a pan. Bring to a boil, cook for 5 minutes, and then lower the heat to a simmer. Add the apple, pear, and all the dried fruit, cover, and simmer for 45 minutes to 1 hour or until tender.

Transfer to a bowl and add the lychees. Heat the sake and, just as it comes to a boil, pour it over the fruits, stir, and serve.

sake is a complicated subject and, like wine, it varies in quality. Most are delicious, however, and you need to experiment to find those that you prefer. Sake is served both warm and cold, the latter being the preferred route for most westerners when it is often compared to a dry fino sherry.

fruit yakitori

with lime syrup

½ cup water

½ cup white sugar

juice and zest of 2 limes

½ pineapple, cut into 1-inch chunks
   (or use canned pineapple chunks)

2 bananas, cut into 1½-inch pieces

3 kiwi fruit, peeled and quartered

4 bamboo skewers, soaked in cold water for 2 hours

Put the water, half the sugar, and the lime juice and zest in a small pan. Bring to a boil, lower the heat, and simmer gently for 10–15 minutes or until thick and syrupy. Set aside.

Thread the fruit onto the skewers. Scatter the remaining sugar evenly over them. Heat a grill pan or broiler and cook until the fruit is golden and slightly charred, turning occasionally. Drizzle with the lime syrup.

sake poached pears

with warm chocolate sauce

2½ cups water

½ cup sake

1 cup plus 2 tablespoons white sugar

2 star anise

1 cinnamon stick

juice and zest of 1 lime

2 ripe but firm Chinese pears, peeled
   but left whole

for the chocolate sauce

⅔ cup heavy cream

¼ cup (½ stick) butter

3 ounces dark chocolate

white sugar, to taste

zest of 1 lime

Put the water, sake, sugar, star anise, cinnamon, lime juice and zest in a small, deep saucepan and bring to a boil. Simmer vigorously for 5 minutes, then lower the heat to a gentle simmer. Add the pears, cover, and simmer for about 45 minutes, or until tender. Remove from the heat and let cool in the liquor.

To make the sauce, place all the ingredients except the lime zest in a small pan and heat gently until melted and smooth. Stir in the lime zest.

To serve, place the cooked pears on a cutting board, cut each one in half, and remove and discard the core. Place in 2 serving bowls and pour the chocolate sauce over them.

The poaching needs to be gentle, the objective being not just to soften the pears, but to infuse them with the spicy delights of star anise and cinnamon. Other spices that work well are cloves and cardamoms but don't be tempted to go over-board, or you'll end up with something rather confused.

the chocolate needs to be of good quality; dark and forbidding but full of complex flavors. There is something about spicy food that makes chocolate seem a popular way to finish.

green tea drizzle cake

with crème fraîche

serves 6–8

¾ cup all-purpose flour

½ ounce green tea powder (optional)

½ teaspoon baking powder

½ cup sugar

4 eggs

⅓ cup (¾ stick) butter, melted and cooled

crème fraîche (or sour cream), for serving

for the green tea syrup

2 tablespoons green tea leaves

⅔ cup boiling water

⅔ cup caster sugar

Preheat the oven to 350°F. Grease an 8-inch round cake pan and dust it with flour.

Sift the flour, green tea powder (if using), and baking powder into a large bowl. Put the sugar and eggs into a large heatproof bowl over a pan of barely simmering water. Using an electric beater, beat the sugar and eggs for 2–3 minutes until the mixture triples in volume, lightens in color, and is the consistency of lightly whipped cream.

Sift the flour mixture into the sugar and eggs, and drizzle the melted butter down the side of the bowl, then gently fold in until incorporated. The batter should not be beaten or overworked. Pour into the prepared pan. Bake on the bottom shelf of the oven for 30–35 minutes, or until the cake is golden and firm to the touch and coming away from the side of the pan. A skewer inserted into the center should come out clean.

While the cake is cooking, make the green tea syrup. Stir the green tea leaves into the boiling water and let stand for 2–3 minutes to create a strong infusion. Strain the tea into a small pan with the sugar and set it over a very low heat until the sugar has completely dissolved. Increase the heat and boil rapidly for 5 minutes until you have a light syrup. Remove 3–4 tablespoons of the syrup and set aside to cool. Keep the rest of the syrup warm while the cake is cooking.

As soon as the cake is baked, remove from the oven but leave in the pan for a few minutes to cool slightly. Skewer the cake surface and drizzle the warm syrup slowly and evenly over the top of the cake. Let it cool completely in the pan. Mix the cooled reserved syrup with the crème fraîche, then cover and chill.

Remove the cake from the pan and peel away the greaseproof paper. Serve with a spoonful of green-tea-spiked crème fraîche.

10
juices
and drinks

Beverages on the wagamama menu are diverse and varied. We serve lots of raw juices—both fruit and vegetable—as well as beer, wine, soft drinks, and, of course, tea. The tea is green, the color a result of the leaves being steamed before they are dried, which prevents them turning black.

We make a lot of our juices, as much for their flavor as for their healthy attributes. All are refreshing, some (like the carrot juice) are spiced with a little ginger, while others are left plain and natural, like the fruit juice blend of apple, orange, and passionfruit.

To make these juices, you do need a dedicated juicer. These vary quite a lot in price and it may be worth considering a cheaper model while you experiment to see how frequently you come to use one. The quantities here are for one large or two small glasses.

Many diners in the restaurants start with a fresh juice and then move on to tea, but a great number also have a soft drink or beer.

Most of our beers are from the East. They tend to have an alcohol rating around the 5 percent mark, which ensures a strength of character sufficient to cope with the food. A lower-alcohol beer can be drowned out by the strong flavors of the food and this is also true of softer beers, like pale ales.

Wines are chosen to complement the food, so the whites tend to be dry and crisp or quite full-flavored and fragrant to stand up to the spicing. On the red front, light and fruity works best —anything too tannic tends to clash with the spices. Sake is also popular and highlights the need for a wine with quite a distinct flavor, so leave the delicate bottles for another time.

Green tea is probably the most traditional of all the drinks we serve. This is a large subject and not something that can be covered in enough detail here. Suffice to say that there are a number of different grades of green tea and a great deal of ceremony associated with drinking it.

What is best to drink with the dishes in this book is purely a matter of preference. And while the idea of not drinking when eating can seem odd, given the amount written about pairing food with suitable beverages, it is a route well worth trying. Consider a bowl of wagamama *ramen* by itself and then sit and relax over a cup of green tea. The world can seem a better place.

pineapple and watermelon juice

6 ounces pineapple, peeled, cored, and cut into cubes
6 ounces watermelon flesh
small handful of cilantro, including stalks
½ red chile, trimmed, seeded, and cut in half
¼ cup orange juice

Push all the ingredients through a juicer, stir, and pour into 2 glasses.

raw juice

We wondered how the raw juice would be received when we first put it on the menu.
Its name seems almost too healthy, but it has walked out the door from the first day
it went on sale.

1 apple, peeled, cored, and cut in half
1 scant cup orange juice
1 tomato, cored
2-inch piece of cucumber, roughly chopped
4 medium carrots, peeled and finely chopped

Push all the ingredients through a juicer, stir, and pour into 2 glasses.

*Above left: pineapple and
watermelon juice.
Above right: raw juice.*

apple and cranberry juice

A good juicer tends to generate a rather attractive froth, which sits on the top of the juice much like milk on a cappuccino. The staff have competitions to see how perfect they can make the froth.

6 apples, peeled, cored, and cut in half
1 cup cranberries

Push the apples and cranberries through a juicer and pour into 2 glasses.

carrot juice

2-inch piece of fresh ginger root, peeled and roughly chopped
6 medium carrots, peeled and finely sliced

Push the ingredients through a juicer and pour into 2 glasses.

Below left: apple and cranberry juice.
Below right: carrot juice.

apple and orange juice

4 apples, peeled, cored, and cut in half
1 cup orange juice

Push the apples through a juicer, combine with the orange juice, and pour into 2 glasses.

apple, carrot, and watercress

4 apples, peeled, cored, and cut in half
2 handfuls of watercress, washed
4 medium carrots, peeled and finely chopped

Push the apples, then the watercress, and finally the carrots through a juicer and pour into 2 glasses.

apple, passionfruit, and orange juice

1 passionfruit
4 apples, peeled, cored, and cut in half
1 cup orange juice

Cut the passionfruit in half, scoop out the seeds and pulp, and push it with the apples through a juicer. Combine with the orange juice and pour into 2 glasses.

apple, carrot, and celery juice

4 medium carrots, peeled and finely chopped
2 celery stalks, finely sliced
3 apples, peeled, cored, and cut in half

Push all the ingredients through a juicer and pour into 2 glasses.

apple, celery, and mint juice

6 apples, peeled, cored, and cut in half
2 sprigs of mint (including stalks), roughly chopped
2 celery stalks, finely sliced

Push all the ingredients through a juicer and pour into 2 glasses.

Sales of juices have rocketed in recent years. It used to be tea, beer, soft drinks, and then wine, but now juices top the list. Customers say they like the flavor and the healthy aspect and undoubtedly you tend to feel rather pleased with yourself after drinking something packed so full of goodness.

index

author acknowledgements

Of the very many people who helped in the process of this book I would especially like to thank Paul O'Farrell, who initially commissioned the project and then had the vision to sit back and watch it happen; to Kyle Cathie, who has a canny sense of the creative; Ian Neill who loomed large at all the right moments and Jay Travis, who managed to enthuse and teach me about cricket at the same time.

A book like this is very much a team project and I would like to thank Sarah Epton, Vanessa Courtier, Joss Herd, Deirdre Rooney and Wei Tang, all of whom influenced the project hugely.

The staff at wagamama were all enormously helpful, particularly the head chefs worldwide – Australia, Holland, Ireland and the UK – who contributed recipes and suggestions with enthusiasm. To Adrian McCormack, Lisa King, Andreas Karlsson, Dinah Meister, Peter Hill, Sarah Crawford, Mark Tilson, Gary Virdee and Milroy Cruize for early insights which were crucial. The task of transferring recipes from restaurant kitchen to domestic setting was greatly assisted by Jason Pettit, whose unfailing good humour got us through most of the hurdles with a smile. To Vikki O'Neill, who has perfected the art of the possible like no one else.

My agent Ivan Mulcahy, whose calm head stilled choppy waters with Celtic charm.

My greatest debt, as ever, is to my wife Sue, who wielded chopsticks, slurped noodles, gave me space and played full-time mum to Tom and Ruby for more months than she should have.